# About the Cover

Authoritarian rule has been a core feature of life for many of Africa's peoples—as it has for many populations across the globe. As readers of this book will see, though, Africa's experience of authoritarianism has been complex and profoundly shaped by multiple factors including Western colonialism and imperialism, in addition to what could be considered distinctively "African" ideas and experiences. While some authoritarian ideals have at times resonated with some African communities, most notably the tendency to prioritize order and stability, others have been—and continue to be—fiercely contested. It should therefore be clear from the pages that follow that there is nothing inherently authoritarian about African politics. And while it is always tempting to speak of "Africa," in reality the experiences of different countries has varied markedly, both in terms of the quality of democracy and the nature of authoritarian rule. We have tried to capture this complexity and variety in the book's subtitle: Repression, Resistance, and the Power of Ideas.

Our cover photo is an attempt to capture some of these ambiguities. The military has played a central role in maintaining authoritarian rule in many parts of the continent, both during the colonial era and subsequently. Indeed, the military 'strongman' is one of the hackneyed clichés of African politics still found in parts of the Western media and wider zeitgeist. The cover photo tries to communicate how much more complicated the picture is. For while the soldiers in the photo are from an authoritarian state governed by a former rebel leader—Burundi—they are also serving in an African Union peacekeeping mission, in Somalia. Thus while at home they may represent, at least in part, the implementing arm of a violent, authoritarian regime, elsewhere on the continent they form—at least in theory—part of a much more positive and aspirational vision of African leadership.

AFRICAN WORLD HISTORIES

# *Authoritarian Africa*

# AFRICAN WORLD HISTORIES

*Series Editor*
**Trevor R. Getz,** San Francisco State University

African World Histories is a series of retellings of some of the most commonly discussed episodes of the African and global past from the perspectives of Africans who lived through them. Accessible yet scholarly, African World Histories gives students insights into African experiences concerning many of the events and trends that are commonly discussed in the history classroom.

## Titles in the Series

**Published**

*Cosmopolitan Africa, 1700–1875*
Trevor R. Getz, San Francisco State University

*Colonial Africa, 1884–1994*
Dennis Laumann, University of Memphis

*Sovereignty and Struggle, 1945–1994*
Jonathan T. Reynolds, Northern Kentucky University

*Africanizing Democracies, 1980–Present*
Alicia Decker, Pennsylvania State University
Andrea Arrington, Indiana State University

*Bantu Africa: 3500 BCE to the Present*
Catherine Cymone Fourshey, Bucknell University
Rhonda Gonzalez, University of Texas at San Antonio
Christina Saidi, Kutztown University

AFRICAN WORLD HISTORIES

# *Authoritarian Africa*

## Repression, Resistance, and the Power of Ideas

## Nic Cheeseman
*University of Birmingham*

## Jonathan Fisher
*University of Birmingham*

New York    Oxford
OXFORD UNIVERSITY PRESS

Oxford University Press is a department of the University of Oxford.
It furthers theUniversity's objective of excellence in research, scholarship,
and education by publishing worldwide. Oxford is a registered trade mark of
Oxford University Press in the UK and certain other countries.

Published in the United States of America by Oxford University Press
198 Madison Avenue, New York, NY 10016, United States of America.

For titles covered by Section 112 of the US Higher Education
Opportunity Act, please visit www.oup.com/us/he for the latest
information about pricing and alternate formats.

**Library of Congress Cataloging-in-Publication Data**

Names: Cheeseman, Nic, 1979- author. | Fisher, Jonathan, 1985- author.
Title: Authoritarian Africa : repression, resistance, and the power of
    ideas / Nic Cheeseman, Jonathan Fisher.
Other titles: African world histories.
Description: New York ; Oxford : Oxford University Press, 2019. | Series:
    African world histories | Includes index. | Summary: "A higher education
    history textbook on the history of authoritarianism in Africa"—
    Provided by publisher.
Identifiers: LCCN 2019027564 (print) | LCCN 2019027565 (ebook) | ISBN
    9780190279653 (paperback) | ISBN 9780190062699 (epub) | ISBN
    9780190072667 (ebook)
Subjects: LCSH: Authoritarianism—Africa. | Democratization—Africa. |
    Africa—Politics and government—1960-
Classification: LCC JQ1875 .C56 2019  (print) | LCC JQ1875  (ebook) | DDC
    320.96—dc23
LC record available at https://lccn.loc.gov/2019027564
LC ebook record available at https://lccn.loc.gov/2019027565

Printing number: 9  8  7  6  5  4  3  2  1
Printed by LSC Communications, Inc., United States of America

*This book is dedicated to all those in Africa and beyond who have dedicated their lives to fighting for justice, human rights, and freedom.*

# CONTENTS

List of Boxes, Figures, Maps, and Tables   xi

Acknowledgments   xiii

About the Authors   xv

Series Introduction   xvii

Introduction   xix

Chapter 1  The Defeat of Democracy   1

The Colonial Legacy   5
Big-Man Politics   9
Conclusion: Understanding Fragile Authoritarianism   16
References   17
Suggested Readings   18

Chapter 2  Between Tradition and Modernity   19

Authoritarian Typologies in the Postindependence Era   21
The Power of Ideas   29
Freedom   35
Conclusion: Performing Power   42
References   43
Suggested Readings   44

Chapter 3  It's the Economy, Stupid!   45

Oil and the Politics of Survival   48
Trade Unions and Political Bargaining in Zambia   53
Conclusion: The Impact of Natural Resources   57
References   59
Suggested Readings   59

Chapter 4  The Tail Wagging the Dog?   61

Foreign Aid and the Cold War: 1975–1990   66
The Fall of the Berlin Wall and the Rise of Political
    Conditionality: 1989–1994   70

Authoritarian Survival and International Politics: 1990–2005   **75**
Conclusion: Does the Tail Wag the Dog?   **79**
References   **80**
Suggested Readings   **81**

## Chapter 5  Authoritarian Rule 2.0   82

Electoral Authoritarianism   **86**
Developmental Authoritarianism   **90**
Is Authoritarianism "Better" Than Democracy?   **97**
Conclusion: The Power of Labels   **103**
References   **105**
Suggested Readings   **106**

## Conclusion   107

## Key Terms and Concepts   131

## Index   135

# List of Boxes, Figures, Maps, and Tables

## Boxes

Box I.1 World's Current Longest-Serving Leaders
(September 2019)     xxi
Box I.2 Anthems and Praise Songs in Honor of
President Jammeh     xxiv
Box I.3 Articulating Authoritarianism     xxvi
Box 1.1 The Ghanaian National Anthem     2
Box 1.2 Chiefs and Traditional Leaders     3
Box 1.3 Settler Colonialism     8
Box 1.4 Colonial Variations: Belgian, British, French,
and Portuguese Rule in Africa     10
Box 1.5 African Responses to Colonial Rule     12
Box 2.1 Women Leaders in Authoritarian Africa     23
Box 2.2 Military Coups in Postcolonial Africa     25
Box 2.3 Titles Used by African Authoritarian Leaders     33
Box 2.4 The African National Congress and the
Freedom Charter     37
Box 3.1 Theft, Excess, and Impunity in Africa's
Gatekeeper States     52
Box 3.2 Life in a Petro-State     58
Box 4.1 Somalia's Cold War International Relations     63
Box 4.2 From China to Cuba: The Cold War in Africa     68
Box 4.3 The Era of Political Conditionality     72
Box 4.4 The "Afterlives" of African Authoritarians—
And Their Parties     76
Box 5.1 "Revolutionary Presidents"     94
Box 5.2 The Challenge of Promoting Gender Equality     98
Box 5.3 Time for "African Democracy"?     100
Box C.1 Education for Self-Reliance     112
Box C.2 The African Union     122

## Figures

3.1 The value of crude oil, 1983–2013 (price per barrel
in current US$)     50
3.2 GDP per capita in selected countries (1961–91),
current US$     56

4.1  Zambian ballot paper from one-party state era          73
5.1  The world's fastest growing economies in 2017          91
C.1  Support for democracy in Africa 2016–18               110
C.2  Trends in African democracy, 1990–2015               128

## MAPS

1.1  Location of African capital cities, 2016               6
C.1  Distribution of national resources in Africa, 2008    126

## TABLES

2.1  Range of political regimes in Africa in the 1970s,
     selected examples                                      22
3.1  Major Oil Producers and Political Freedom, 1975–2005   49
5.1  The African "Menu of Manipulation"                    87

## IMAGES

C.1  Resistance and memory in Zimbabwe                     115
C.2  Gado's cartoon of the 2017 Kenyan presidential election  116

# Acknowledgments

Writing a book is a complex process, and so even a relatively short volume represents a collaborative effort. In putting together *African Authoritarianism: Repression, Resistance, and the Power of Ideas*, we have therefore been fortunate to have enjoyed the support of a great editorial and administrative team. Trevor R. Getz was a constant source of encouragement, insight, and enthusiasm, while Charles Cavaliere offered sound advice and regular encouragement right to the end. We would also like to thank Anna Russell and Anna Fitzsimons and others at Oxford University Press for their hard work in bringing this project to fruition, and our excellent doctoral student, Daniel Munday, who proofread the text.

The argument that we present here was developed during 2018, but it draws on numerous conversations, seminars, fieldwork trips, and interviews that we have engaged in over the last decade. We therefore owe thanks to many hundreds of people, especially those who have made time to talk to us in Djibouti, Eritrea, Ethiopia, Kenya, Malawi, Nigeria, Rwanda, Somalia, South Africa, South Sudan, Sudan, Tanzania, Uganda, Zambia, and Zimbabwe—often at not inconsiderable risk to their own safety. Although this book was not envisaged at the time, it was their insight and evidence that made it possible. Closer to home, we would also like to thank our colleagues who, first at the African Studies Centre of the University of Oxford, and more recently at the International Development Department (IDD) of the University of Birmingham, provided the intellectual stimulation and collegial solidarity that academic endeavor requires.

As is so often the case, the process of refining our thoughts and clarifying our ideas involved first discussing them with colleagues and then benefitting from the generous time given by reviewers. In our case, we are very grateful to the individuals whose constructive and thorough suggestions helped us to significantly strengthen this manuscript: Saheed Aderinto, Western Carolina University; Andrea Arrington, North Carolina School of Science and Mathematics; Jesse Bucher, Roanoke College; Alicia C. Decker, Pennsylvania State

University; Corrie Decker, University of California, Davis; John W. Harbeson, City University of New York; Carl LeVan, American University; Amanda Lewis-Nang'ea, State University of New York at Geneseo; and, Peter VonDoepp, University of Vermont. Any remaining errors are ours alone.

The other important component of the revision process was the feedback we received from students on early versions of our argument. In this regard we were particularly lucky to be able to road test much of the analysis that follows on the engaged and thoughtful IDD master's students who took the Development Politics (2017/2018 & 2018/2019), Authoritarianism and Development (2018/2019) and Democracy and Development (2018/2019) modules. Teaching these classes was a real pleasure, and we got back more than we gave.

# About the Authors

**Nic Cheeseman** is Professor of Democracy and International Development at the University of Birmingham and was formerly the Director of the African Studies Centre at Oxford University. He mainly works on democracy, elections, and development and has conducted fieldwork in a range of African countries, including Ghana, Kenya, Malawi, Nigeria, Uganda, Zambia, and Zimbabwe. The articles that he has published based on this research have won a number of prizes, including the GIGA award for the best article in Comparative Area Studies (2013) and the Frank Cass Award for the best article in Democratization (2015), and in 2019 he was awarded the Joni Lovenduski Prize for outstanding professional achievement by a midcareer scholar by the Political Studies Association of the UK. Professor Cheeseman is also the author or editor of ten books, including *Democracy in Africa* (2015), *Institutions and Democracy in Africa* (2017), *How to Rig an Election* (2018), and *Coalitional Presidentialism in Comparative Perspective* (2018). In addition, he is the founding editor of the *Oxford Encyclopedia of African Politics*, a former editor of the journal *African Affairs*, and an advisor to, and writer for, Kofi Annan's African Progress Panel. A frequent commentator on African and global events, Professor Cheeseman's analysis has appeared in the *Economist*, *Le Monde*, *Financial Times*, *Newsweek*, the *Washington Post*, *New York Times*, *BBC*, and *Daily Nation*, and he writes a regular column for the *Mail & Guardian*. In total, his articles have been read over a million times. Many of his interviews and insights can be found on the website that he founded and coedits, www.democracyinafrica.org.

**Jonathan Fisher** is Reader in African Politics in, and Director of, the International Development Department at the University of Birmingham. He is also a Research Fellow in the Centre for Gender and Africa Studies at the University of the Free State and Academic Director of the Governance and Social Development Resource Centre. A political scientist by training, Jonathan's research focuses on the intersection between authoritarian rule, political transformation, and in/security in Africa, and he is particularly interested in the politics of "postliberation" states. His work has been funded by the Arts and Humanities Research Council (AHRC), British Academy, Economic and Social Research Council (ESRC), Facebook, and the Newton Fund and has seen him conduct research across the African continent, from Eritrea to Nigeria and from Kenya to South Africa.

# Series Introduction

The African World Histories series presents a new approach to teaching and learning for African history and African studies courses. Its main innovation is to interpret African and global experiences from the perspectives of the Africans who lived through them. By integrating accounts and representations produced or informed by Africans with accessible scholarly analysis at both local and global levels, African World Histories gives students insight into Africans' understandings and experiences of such episodes as the Atlantic slave trade, the growth of intercontinental commerce and the Industrial Revolution, colonialism, and the Cold War. The authors in this series look at these episodes through the lenses of culture, politics, social organization, daily life, and economics in an integrated format informed by recent scholarly studies as well as primary source materials. Unlike those of many textbooks and series, the authors of African World Histories actively take positions on major questions, such as the centrality of violence in the colonial experience, the cosmopolitan nature of precolonial African societies, and the importance of democratization in Africa today. Underlying this approach is the belief that students can succeed when presented with relatively brief, jargon-free interpretations of African societies that integrate Africans' perspectives with critical interpretations and that balance intellectual rigor with broad accessibility.

This series is designed for use in both the world history and the African history/studies classroom. As an African history/studies teaching tool, it combines continentwide narratives with emphases on specific, localized, and thematic stories that help demonstrate wider trends. As auxiliary texts for the world history classroom, the volumes in this series can help to illuminate important episodes in the global past from the perspectives of Africans, adding complexity and depth, as well as facilitating intellectual growth for students. Thus, it will help world history students not only understand that the human past was "transnational" and shared, but also see how it was understood differently by different groups and individuals.

African World Histories is the product of a grand collaboration. The authors include scholars from around the world and across Africa. Each volume is reviewed by multiple professionals in African history and related fields. The excellent team of editors at Oxford University Press, led by Charles Cavaliere, put a great deal of effort into commissioning, reviewing, and bringing these volumes to publication. Finally, we all stand on the shoulders of early giants in the field, including Cheikh Anta Diop, Joseph Ki-Zerbo, Jan Vansina, and Roland Oliver.

**—TREVOR R. GETZ, SERIES EDITOR**

# Introduction

## *Authoritarian Africa*

On December 1, 2016, for the first time in its post-independence history, the small West African **state** of The Gambia looked to be on the verge of changing leaders through the ballot box.

In power since leading a successful military coup in July 1994, the country's president Yahya Jammeh—who five years earlier told *BBC* reporters that he would "rule this country for one billion years"— conceded defeat in a result that surprised the world.

Jammeh had overthrown The Gambia's first president, Sir Dawda Jawara, at the age of twenty-nine, accusing him of corruption and **authoritarianism**. Despite promising to right these wrongs, he subsequently set about instituting his own, brutal dictatorship—suspending the constitution, restricting press freedoms, building a **surveillance state**, closing newspapers, and cracking down on opposition. In December 2011, after winning an election marred by accusations of fraud and intimidation, Jammeh dismissed critics of his regime, saying "I will not bow down before anybody . . . and if they don't like that they can go to hell!" In the lead-up to the next election, the president backed up his words by arresting an opposition leader and disrupting pro-democracy protests, declaring that "I will never tolerate opposition to destabilize this country." However, when it became clear that he had lost the election—by a 43.3 percent to 39.6 percent margin— Jammeh stunned the African and international media by congratulating his opponent on his victory. In a televised message, he wished his successor "all the best" and assured him that "you are the elected president of The Gambia. I have no ill will."

This moment of democratic humility was not, however, to last. Days later, Jammeh retracted his concession, demanding that the election be rerun and arguing that there had been "serious . . . abnormalities" in the election process—a process he had, days earlier, referred to as the "most transparent, rig-proof elections in the whole world." In the face of regional and international condemnation, he appealed to

The Gambia's Supreme Court to nullify the result and declared a state of emergency—endorsed by the country's National Assembly—which extended his rule for a further three months. A concerted regional effort to dislodge him, which culminated in an invasion by Senegalese forces under the mandate of a regional mission entitled "Operation Restore Democracy," nevertheless saw Jammeh finally agree to leave and his successor—Adama Barrow—sworn in as The Gambia's third president in January 2017.

For some, this episode represented a cautionary tale for Africa's authoritarian leaders in the twenty-first century: the idea that their time in power is coming to a close and that the days of the one-party state and the "president for life" are over. Those who believe that **multiparty elections** naturally lead, over time, to transfers of power and higher levels of democracy rushed to cite Jammeh as evidence for their thesis. The fact that important regional organizations such as the African Union—an association of fifty-five African states that was originally founded in 1963 to fight colonialism and defend the sovereignty and independence of African states—refused to recognize Jammeh's government was also interpreted as proof of a growing consensus in favor of democratic norms and values among African leaders.

But there is another interpretation of recent events in The Gambia, which highlights not Jammeh's eventual removal from power but rather his remarkable longevity until that point.

Although he lost the contest, Jammeh had been in power for some twenty-six years and almost 40 percent of those who cast ballots in The Gambia's 2016 presidential election supported him—although this figure is likely to have been inflated through vote rigging. Some of these voters were no doubt too afraid to do otherwise after a quarter century of repression. Such concerns did not, however, deter the 43.3 percent who voted against him. It is also likely that at least a significant minority of the population were persuaded to support him by ties of ethnicity and kinship, his promises of **patronage** and political stability, and cult of personality. Furthermore, while the African Union spoke out in favor of a transfer of power, it had failed to do so over the previous two decades when his government committed numerous human rights abuses. In other words, on closer inspection, events in The Gambia may not represent as resounding a rejection of authoritarian rule as they appear to at first glance.

It is therefore possible to read a very different story into Jammeh's rise and fall—one that emphasizes the ability of authoritarian leaders to retain power for long periods, subverting multiparty elections and (supposedly) democratic constitutions in the process. Following the "third wave" of democratization in the 1990s, discussed later in this study, almost all African countries with the exception of Eritrea began to hold multiparty elections of one kind or another. Yet despite this, there has been remarkably little political change in many countries, in large part because authoritarian leaders have manipulated these processes to their own advantage. As a result, presidents win the vast majority of the elections that they contest (Cheeseman 2015), and less than half of the countries in sub-Saharan Africa have ever removed a government via the ballot box. In some cases, this makes a farce of the claim to democratic legitimacy, as leaders win power with 98 percent of the vote (Rwanda in 2017) or 100 percent of parliamentary seats (Ethiopia in 2015). Given this, it is perhaps not surprising that at the time of writing, the continent features half of the world's ten longest-serving leaders (see Box I.1).

## Box I.1    World's Current Longest-Serving Leaders (September 2019)*

*African leaders are highlighted in bold*

| Name | Title and Country | Years in Power |
|------|-------------------|----------------|
| 1. **Paul Biya** | President of Cameroon | 42 |
| 2. **Teodoro Obiang Nguema Mbasogo** | President of Equatorial Guinea | 38 |
| 3. Ali Khameini | Supreme Leader of Iran | 36 |
| 4. Nursultan Nazarbayev | President of Kazakhstan/Leader of the Nation | 34 |
| 5. Hun Sen | Prime Minister of Cambodia | 33 |
| 6. **Yoweri Museveni** | President of Uganda | 32 |
| 7. **Idris Déby** | President of Chad | 27 |
| 8. **Isaias Afwerki** | President of Eritrea | 26 |
| 9. Emomali Rahmon | President of Tajikistan | 25 |
| 10. Alexander Lukashenko | President of Belarus | 25 |

* Excludes royal figures and leaders with multiple, non-consecutive terms in office.

## UNDERSTANDING AFRICAN AUTHORITARIANISM

African authoritarianism is not, however, a static or easily predictable phenomenon. While a number of authoritarian states have survived for decades despite numerous predictions of imminent collapse, as in Chad, Rwanda, and Zimbabwe, this is not always the case. Instead, some of the continent's more public-spirited presidents have voluntarily retired (Senegal in 1980; Tanzania in 1985), while a small number of entrenched leaders have been forced to stand aside through international and domestic efforts (Malawi in 1994; Burkina Faso in 2014; Sudan in 2019). Moreover, a number of Africa's most democratic polities today were dictatorships of a civilian (Benin, South Africa, Zambia) or military (Ghana, Nigeria) bent until the 1990s.

The collapse of a number of high-profile repressive political systems serves as an important reminder that sustaining authoritarian rule requires constant effort and vigilance. It also involves the construction of a political machine underpinned by effective institutions, whether formal ones like the army, or informal ones, such as personal networks of government loyalists. In Malawi, for example, President-for-Life Hastings Banda entrenched his hold on power by establishing seven different security forces, whose job was both to keep the population in line and to spy on each other in order to root out any disloyalty to His Excellency.

When such a political machine is developed, the departure of an authoritarian leader or regime may not lead to the end of authoritarianism itself. As this book will show, the factors underlying African authoritarianism—in its many shapes and forms since the colonial period—are far too complex to be reduced to the role and personalities of individual leaders or governments. Authoritarian systems are built not just around oppression and fear but also around co-optation and incentives. In most instances, African authoritarian regimes have been sustained by lengthy chains of **patron–client networks** linking the resources of the state to businesses, churches, chiefs, and local politicians, and the presidential mansion to distant villages and communities. The exit of the "**big man**" at the top has often required only a small adjustment for local intermediaries further down the chain, some of whom have perfected the art of accommodation since the colonial era.

Naturally, funding the repression perpetuated by the security forces and maintaining the continued loyalty of clients and populations in authoritarian states has depended somewhat on the resource wealth and **state capacity** of a particular country. A long history of expansive state bureaucracies has enabled successive Ethiopian and Rwandan administrations to maintain a controlling presence in far flung regions in a manner not possible for counterparts in countries like Chad, the Democratic Republic of Congo, and Sudan, where the state's authority has sometimes run barely beyond the capital. Similarly, while resource-poor Malawi and (until recently) Uganda have had to look elsewhere to fund their activities, oil wealth has helped undergird authoritarian systems in Angola, Equatorial Guinea, and Gabon. In Nigeria, it is estimated that oil contributes around US\$77 billion a year to government funds, enabling a number of military dictators to pay the salaries of the security forces and to sustain their personal networks in the 1970s and 1980s.

Authoritarian regimes have also relied heavily on the resources—developmental and military—of international donor countries and organizations, particularly the World Bank, United States, United Kingdom, France, and, increasingly, China. Dependence on international support has, however, been a double-edged sword. Washington, London, Paris, and Beijing have long-backed faltering authoritarian systems for their own interests—and in some cases continue to do so—but have equally encouraged others to fall by engaging in "democracy promotion." More often, though, divisions between international actors have provided opportunities for authoritarian African governments to play powerful states off against one another, gaining access to aid and security assistance in return for their political allegiance. For example, during the Cold War, when the foreign policy of the United States and the Soviet Union was dominated by their rivalry, leaders in the Horn of Africa were able to source weapons and funding by promising to support one side or the other. International patronage has never been more than a temporary solution, however. In the words of Ugandan president Yoweri Museveni (now well into his fourth decade in power), the end of the Cold War "orphaned" many African dictators as the value of "anti-communist" allies fell away for policymakers in Western capitals. As a result, many authoritarian leaders were left to fend for themselves and had to become more creative.

Despite the significance of repression and patronage to the ability of authoritarian regimes to stay in power, it would therefore be a mistake to assume that dictators must be abhorred by all of their peoples, or that the only strategies they use to power are to buy support and oppress their populations. Authoritarian governments need not be unpopular—at least not with all aspects of society—if they deliver public services and use narratives and ideas that resonate with the country's past, especially if these are communicated through government policies, or by sponsoring artists to communicate their message through popular culture (see Box I.2). Indeed, deeply authoritarian governments in countries such as Ethiopia and Rwanda have explicitly sought to legitimize their rule with reference to the development that they have provided. Until recently, this proved to be a fairly successful strategy, enabling these regimes to secure the support of key constituencies, and high levels of international aid, despite their democratic failings.

---

### Box I.2 Anthems and Praise Songs in Honor of President Jammeh

*Throughout his time in office, President Jammeh encouraged artists to depict him in a positive light to make himself appear popular, offering financial rewards to those who flattered him while intimidating those who were critical. One way in which he did this was to create a competition for individuals to write an anthem to commemorate the July 22 Revolution—the coup that brought him to power—with the winner promised a prize of 1 million Dalasis (about $20,000). The competition was won by Juma K. Camara, but many others also wrote anthems, such as this one by Fatou Ceesay that was published by www.Africa.gm in December 2008.*

> On July 22nd, a new revolution came into existence
> A revolution called the
> Alliance for Patriotic Reorientation and Construction (APRC)
> A party for success
> President Yahya Jammeh a great leader
> President Jammeh, the lion of The Gambia
> The lion who roars for peace, development and prosperity
> With an astonishing goal you've made Gambians proud
> Your extraordinary targets made Gambia what it is
> North, south, east, west, salutes you
> For your greatness.

*This version of the anthem is available at*
*http://africa.gm/africa/article/july-22nd-anthem*

*The practice of sponsoring anthems and praise songs continued throughout Jammeh's rule. In the 2016 general election, the praise song Mansa Douri Mani (Leader Among Leaders) by Samba Bah (Mr Dourl Dourl) was used to support the president's candidacy. In the song, Bah compares Jammeh to revered African leaders such as Thomas Sankara and great international leaders such as Martin Luther King. The song was accompanied by a high-quality video, in which the tune plays in the background while an educated American sounding voice recounts the president's supposed virtues, emphasizing his commitment to development and equality. The lyrics of the song are explicitly designed to position Jammeh in the pantheon of great civil rights campaigners and African revolutionaries.*

*You can watch the video for yourself at*
*https://www.youtube.com/watch?v=8Rd2J02DozY*

In addition to explaining how authoritarian governments survive, this book also emphasizes the legacies of authoritarian rule and how deeply ambiguous and contradictory these often are. African authoritarianism is not, and has never been, simply the prelude to—or absence of—democracy. The discussion so far should also have made it clear that successful authoritarian systems have rarely been based solely on patronage and oppression. Instead, they have often been built around ideas and logics which tap into powerful historical narratives and experiences that often resonate with their people. Notions of "national unity" lay at the heart of the one-party states set up by nationalist movements in Kenya, Malawi, Tanzania, and Zambia in the aftermath of independence, just as liberation from colonial overlords and abusive tyrants has been a core legitimizing narrative of authoritarian governments in Ethiopia, Uganda, and Zimbabwe in more recent years. Similarly, military takeovers in Ghana, Mali, Nigeria, and Sudan from the 1960s to the present day have been premised upon rooting out the corruption and misrule of self-interested, political elites. In Eritrea and South Sudan, national identity has become so intertwined with the secessionist wars fought by the ruling party against Ethiopia and Sudan, respectively, that these movements are viewed by many as having earned—through their blood and sacrifice—the "right to rule."

## Box I.3    Articulating Authoritarianism

This book discusses a wide range of authoritarian regimes in sub-Saharan Africa, from Angola to Zimbabwe. What all of these states have in common is that they deny their citizens a range of political rights and civil liberties. With the exception of Eritrea, they also all combine elements of repression with tightly controlled multiparty elections, which is why many academics refer to them as being "electoral authoritarian," "semidemocratic," or "counterfeit democracies."

At the same time as sharing many similarities, the states we discuss also *vary considerably* in terms of how authoritarian they are. Some, such as Sudan, are particularly brutal and have used strategies such as targeted assassinations of opposition leaders and ethnic cleansing of rival communities. Others, like the civilian one-party states that operated in Senegal, Tanzania, and Zambia during the 1970s and 1980s, were more open and allowed a greater degree of criticism and debate. We use the term "authoritarian" to describe all of these states, but it is important to keep in mind that this does not mean that they were—or are—all the same. Nor should it be assumed that all democratic states—in Africa and beyond—uphold and protect those rights denied to citizens in authoritarian polities. Some authoritarian systems are more open than others, just as some democratic systems are more closed than others (Decker and Arrington 2015).

Elsewhere, authoritarian government has been defended as a much-needed stabilization mechanism to restore order to countries in the aftermath of war, civil conflict, or national trauma. As part of this public relations exercise, democratic or multiparty political systems have regularly been described by African autocrats as "un-African" and depicted as the trigger for bloodshed. In June 1990, Kenyan president Daniel arap Moi, who had ruled the country in a one-party state since 1978, defended his brand of authoritarianism by arguing that "multiparties will create tribalism and divide people on ethnic lines . . . agents of multiparties are still mentally colonized." A similar logic informed Uganda's introduction in 1986 of "no-party democracy"—criticized by a growing number as de facto single-party rule until its disestablishment in 2005. These justifying ideologies may represent, to some extent, the cynical propaganda of authoritarian leaders seeking to legitimate their rule, and this is clearly true of the kind of praise song featured in Box I.2. However, as Claude Ake has argued (2000), when cleverly implemented, they also resonate with many people who look to their governments—first and foremost—to preserve peace and stability.

This book aims to unpack and explain the key factors which have contributed to the persistence and durability of authoritarian rule in Africa since 1945. In doing so, it introduces readers to the variety of authoritarian regimes that have existed across the continent over the last seven decades—including one-party states, military rule, and personal dictatorships—and focuses on five central issues which have facilitated authoritarian government. These are state capacity; patron–client politics; resource wealth; legitimizing narratives; and international support. The book also considers the complex legacies of authoritarian rule for contemporary Africa. We show that understanding the form that authoritarian government has taken, even in countries that are now democratic, is important not just for our sense of the past but also for how we think about and understand the present and the future.

# CONCEPTUALIZING AUTHORITARIANISM

Given all these complexities, it is perhaps not surprising that authoritarianism has proven to be a difficult concept to define and has often been linked to particular contexts. When generalizing, scholars have tended to highlight the degree to which power is centralized and personalized in authoritarian systems, often around one person—usually a president, prime minister or monarch. They have also emphasized the divergence between how the state's power is formally established—how it is *meant* to be exercised—and how it is actually applied. Legally, authoritarian states usually subscribe to the separation of powers: the preeminence of the rule of law, and respect for freedom of expression and organization. In practice, though, they are characterized by overmighty presidents who maintain excessive control over all branches of government, enforce the arbitrary suspension or uneven application of laws, and implement unpredictable crackdowns on perceived opponents—sometimes within the confines of the law, sometimes outside it. The long-term dominance of a particular leader or movement has also been a staple of many authoritarian regimes, as has the use of violence to impose order and suppress dissent.

However, for many theorists, it is not consistency that marks out an authoritarian regime, but rather caprice. In other words, it is the extent to which the realms of law, politics, and security are subjected to the particular desires of a leader or ruling clique without check or contradiction that indicates the degree of authoritarianism. Author and novelist Christopher Hitchens perhaps came closest to capturing the core of this interpretation of authoritarianism in his 2010 memoirs when he argued that:

> The true essence of a dictatorship is not—in fact—its regularity, but its unpredictability and caprice; those who live under it must never be able to relax, must never be quite sure if they have followed the rules or not (Hitchens 2010: 51).

In this regard, political scientists Juan Linz and Alfred Stepan—drawing on the work of nineteenth-century sociologist Max Weber—have underlined "sultanism" as being at the extreme end of the authoritarian spectrum (Linz and Stepan 1996). "Sultanistic" regimes are those where rulers exercise almost complete and absolute authority and where tolerance of opposition or criticism is permitted or withdrawn entirely at their pleasure. Such was the form of authoritarianism exercised by Idi Amin of Uganda between 1971 and 1979 and "Emperor" Jean-Bedel Bokassa of the Central African Republic between 1966 and 1979.

In 1982, during the heyday of "big man" authoritarian rule in Africa, scholars Robert Jackson and Carl Rosberg sought to delineate typologies of this kind of "personal rule," characterizing African leaders into four different categories. The first, princes, are rulers who maintain power through manipulating the rivalries of ambitious oligarchs and elites, such as Senegal's Léopold Senghor. The second, autocrats, are akin to an **absolute monarch** who commands the country as if it were "his estate." Third is a small number of rulers—including Ghana's Kwame Nkrumah—who they argued were "prophets," driven by ideas and a desire to reshape their countries according to a particular ideology. The final type of personal ruler is the tyrant; similar to Linz and Stepan's "sultans," the tyrant exercises power "in a completely arbitrary fashion" according to his impulses alone (Jackson and Rosberg 1982).

To date, "sultanistic" systems have been relatively rare in Africa, as have "totalitarian" regimes—a concept applied by Hannah Arendt and others to the authoritarian regimes of Nazi Germany and Stalin's USSR—where the government seeks to maintain "total" control over all areas of life, from popular culture to high politics (Arendt 1951). More commonly, African authoritarianism has mixed elements of formal democracy and predictable, bureaucratic governance with personalized rule and the dominance of informalized power structures in which an individual's power is based not simply on the position that s/he occupies but on her/his personal relationship with the ruling family and elite. As a result, many scholars have understood African authoritarianism in terms of its "**hybridity**"—both in terms of the way in which it mixes elements of democracy, such as elections, with high levels of repression, and because it draws its authority from a combination of the charismatic appeal of the leader and the bureaucratic authority of formal rules and regulations.

This does not mean that these two systems exist independently, or that ministries and formal state offices are simply hollow edifices behind which lie shadowy networks wielding ultimate control. The two are part of a single, complex form of rule and interact unpredictably but constantly—as they have done since the colonial period. Hence, long-serving African autocrats have rarely sought to remain in office or see-off opposition without turning to formal, legal mechanisms—constitutional amendments (albeit secured through bribes and intimidation) or legal appeals (albeit to courts packed with pro-government judges, whose tenure may be abruptly ended if they make the "wrong" judgment).

Often these are exercises in political theatre aimed in large part at an international audience, but in many African countries authoritarian leaders do not hold all the cards. Courts can be overruled, opponents jailed without charge, parliaments turned into rubber stamps, and so forth, but there are also examples of legal mechanisms actually curtailing, sometimes quite unexpectedly, periods of authoritarian leadership. The case of The Gambia described earlier is one example of this; others include the refusal of parliaments to allow presidents to remove presidential term limits—and so extend their stay in office—in Malawi, Nigeria and Zambia during the 2000s.

Such dynamics were common in authoritarian systems led by the nationalists who came to power as the leaders of political parties just before and after independence, and the "insiders" who rose to the top thereafter. They are less frequently found, however, in those authoritarian states established by military officers who seized power by force and often suspended the constitution, ruling by decree. Indeed, recent scholarship on authoritarianism—in Africa and beyond—has emphasized how the way that a regime comes to power—its "launching organization" in the words of political scientist Stephen Haber (2006)—shapes the way that it performs thereafter. Barbara Geddes (2003), for example, has written of the difference between personalist, military, and single-party regimes. Similarly, Beatriz Magaloni has categorized authoritarian states into military, single-party, multiparty, and monarchical systems (2008). These distinctions matter because it is often suggested that because single-party states allow for more political participation and engagement than military regimes, the multiparty systems that emerge out of them are more likely to respect political rights and civil liberties.

While the pages that follow confirm the validity of some of these arguments, it is important to note that the continent poses a number of challenges to such clean-cut classifications, particularly in more recent years when postcolonial nationalists and military regimes have given way to more ambiguous forms of government. Many of the political systems examined in Chapters 4 and 5, for example, are neither fully military nor fully civilian, and often feature elements of personalist or dominant-party rule within a political system that is formally multi-party. In this book, then, we adopt a broad and dynamic understanding of African authoritarianism which considers the phenomenon to be rooted in historical structures and experiences but also constantly evolving as a result of domestic and international circumstances and imperatives.

## STRUCTURE AND APPROACH OF THE BOOK

The chapters that follow explore the history and legacy of authoritarianism in Africa from the colonial era to the present day. In doing so, they are interested not only in the personalities and actions of individual leaders—important as these have often been—but also in the domestic and international structures which have undergirded or undermined their authoritarian systems. While the voices and viewpoints of the elite necessarily loom large across the book—through the inclusion of speeches, newspaper reports, and diplomatic correspondence as primary sources—we have also sought to provide alternative perspectives in many chapters by including broader data drawing on popular song, intellectual responses to authoritarianism, and economic or political indicators. We also reflect on everyday forms of *resistance* to authoritarian rule in the Conclusion. This will enable the reader to analyze some of the trends and trajectories referred to in a different light.

The five chapters of the book are structured chronologically—from the end of the colonial era in Chapter 1 through the present day in Chapter 5. Each chapter, though, focuses on a different factor underlying authoritarian rule in Africa, and the book can therefore also be read thematically. Chapter 1 explores the transformation of colonial states into authoritarian regimes between c.1945 and 1965, underlining the significance of patron–client relationships and state capacity, both in the past and the present. Taking the analysis forward, Chapter 2 looks at the crucial role of ideas in supporting authoritarian systems in Africa, examining the rise of nationalist dictatorships during the 1960s and 1970s and the conflation of ideas of national "unity" with one-party and personal rule—echoes of which can be found in many of today's so-called postliberation regimes.

Chapter 3 builds on this discussion by emphasizing the economic foundations of authoritarian rule and the critical role played by patronage and clientelistic relationships in building popular support. The growing significance of oil, diamonds, international loans, development aid, and other resources for authoritarian regimes during the 1970s and 1980s provides the empirical setting for this chapter. Chapter 4 then addresses the importance of Africa's international relations for the maintenance—or curtailing—of authoritarian rule in many parts of the continent, exploring how the end of the Cold War jeopardized the survival of some governments but provided fresh opportunities to others.

Chapter 5 reflects on the legacy of authoritarianism and examines the impact of authoritarian structures on new democratic political systems. This chapter considers why some African states have been able to resist the post–Cold War continental and international push toward political reform and also reflects on the prospects for democratization in some of Africa's most repressive regimes. The book then concludes with a discussion of the impact of authoritarianism on the lives and attitudes of the African citizens who have lived under it, and what role authoritarianism is likely to play in the continent's future.

## REFERENCES

Ake, Claude. *The Feasibility of Democracy in Africa*. Dakar: CODESRIA, 2000.

Arendt, Hannah. *The Origins of Totalitarianism*. New York: Shocken Books, 1951.

Cheeseman, Nic. *Democracy in Africa: Successes, Failures, and the Struggle for Political Reform*. Cambridge: Cambridge University Press, 2015.

Decker, Alicia C., and Andrea L. Arrington. *Africanizing Democracies: 1980–Present*. New York: Oxford University Press, 2015.

Geddes, Barbara. *Paradigms and Sand Castles: Research Design in Comparative Politics*. Ann Arbor: University of Michigan Press, 2003.

Haber, Stephen. "Authoritarian Government." In *The Oxford Handbook of Political Economy*, edited by Barry Weingast and Donland Wittman, 693–707. New York: Oxford University Press, 2006.

Hitchens, Christopher. *Hitch 22: A Memoir*. London: Atlantic Books, 2010.

Jackson, Robert, and Carl Rosberg. *Personal Rule in Black Africa: Prince, Autocrat, Prophet, Tyrant*. Berkeley: University of California Press, 1982.

Linz, Juan, and Alfred Stephan. *Problems of Democratic Transition and Consolidation: Southern Europe, South America and Post-Communist Europe*. Baltimore, MD: Johns Hopkins University Press, 1996.

Magaloni, Beatriz. "Credible Power-Sharing and the Longevity of Authoritarian Rule." *Comparative Political Studies* 41, nos. 4–5 (2008): 715–741.

## SUGGESTED READINGS

Ezrow, Natasha M., and Erica Frantz. *Dictators and Dictatorships: Understanding Authoritarian Regimes and Their Leaderships*. London: Bloomsbury, 2011.

Herbst, Jeff. *States and Power in Africa: Comparative Lessons in Authority and Control*. Princeton, NJ: Princeton University Press, 2014.

Levitsky, Steven, and Lucan Way. *Competitive Authoritarianism: Hybrid Regimes after the Cold War*. Cambridge: Cambridge University Press, 2010.

Lynch, Gabrielle, and Gordon Crawford. "Democratization in Africa 1990–2010: An Assessment." *Democratization* 18, no. 2 (2011): 275–310.

wa Thiong'o, Ngũgĩ. *Wizard of the Crow*. London: Harvill Secker, 2006.

# The Defeat of Democracy

*Big-Man Rule, the Colonial Legacy,
and Fragile Authoritarianism*

In 1957, Ghana declared independence from the United Kingdom under the leadership of one of the most famous and influential African nationalists of that or any other era, Prime Minister Kwame Nkrumah. The country appeared to be set for an exciting period of economic and political transformation, fueled by its considerable natural resources, most notably gold and cocoa. Nkrumah's Convention People's Party (CPP) was extremely popular and promised to pursue radical social, political, and economic transformation. What is more, the national anthem celebrated the fight against oppression (Box 1.1), and a number of checks and balances had been put in place to prevent the abuse of power, including multiparty elections to determine the government and an independent judiciary. The future looked bright.

Just a few years later, though, everything had changed. The CPP's policies required extending government control over the economy, which angered business leaders and many farmers, while the cost of national transformation exceeded initial expectations and plunged the country into debt. In a bid to consolidate his hold on power amid rising public disapproval, Nkrumah pursued a number of strategies that undermined his democratic credentials. These included

## Box 1.1   The Ghanaian National Anthem

*The music for the Ghanaian national anthem was composed by Mr. Philip Comi Gbeho, a musician and teacher. Like many anthems written around this time, it captures popular hopes for their new country and features a strong commitment to "Freedom for ever, for evermore!" However, much like Ghana's democracy, Gbeho's anthem did not last long. After Nkrumah had been toppled in 1966, the new government kept Gbeho's music but replaced his words with an alternative version—perhaps keen to disassociate themselves from the old regime, which had failed to live up to expectations.*

Lift high the flag of Ghana,
The gay star shining in the sky,
Bright with the souls of our fathers,
Beneath whose shade we'll live and die!
Red for the blood of the heroes in the fight,
Green for the precious farms of our birth-right,
And linked with these the shining golden band
That marks the richness of our Fatherland.

We'll live and die for Ghana, Our land of hope for ages to come! Shout it aloud,
O Ghana,
And beat it upon the drum!
Come from the palm-lined shore, from the broad northern plain,
From the farm and the forest, the mountain and mine.
Your children sing with ancient minstrel lore:
Freedom for ever, for evermore!

God be with us in Ghana
And make our nation great and strong
Brave to defend for ever
The cause of freedom and of right
Forever the flag of Ghana proudly flies
In distant seas or else beneath our skies
Let peace and fellow-feeling be our might
And may our name be a radiant light
This be our vow, O Ghana,
To live as one, in unity, And in your strength, O Ghana,
To build a new fraternity!
Africa waits in the night of the clouded years

For the spreading light that now appears
To give us all a place beneath the sun:
The destined ending of a task well done.

*To listen to the music, go to:*
http://www.nationalanthems.me/ghana-god-bless-our-homeland-ghana/

introducing a Trade Union Act in 1958 that made strikes illegal and extending the CPP's authority over rural areas by subordinating **chiefs** (Box 1.2) to political control. The same year, the Preventative Detention Act enabled the prime minister to detain people without trial for up to five years, confirming the increasingly authoritarian bent of the administration.

## Box 1.2    Chiefs and Traditional Leaders

The term "Chief" usually refers to a leader of an ethnic group or clan whose authority was historically based on lineage or descent rather than merit or election. Sometimes the institution of chieftaincy is referred to in other terms, such as "traditional leadership."

In Africa, chieftaincy is often presented and understood as a precolonial form of authority. In many cases, however, particular chiefly lineages were inaugurated by colonial powers who looked to chiefs to collect taxes and pacify populations on their behalf. During the colonial era, therefore, the powers of chiefs—both pre-existing and "invented" (Ranger 1983)—were significantly enhanced. In some cases, this led to the imposition of "warrant" chiefs within communities that had not previously recognized the legitimacy of centralized authority in order to facilitate the co-optation of particular groups.

Despite the introduction of democratic forms of government in almost all African countries, chiefs continue to wield considerable influence, especially in rural areas. Their roles can include managing communal land, resolving marital disputes, and enforcing customary law. In a small number of countries, such as Ghana, traditional leaders are formally represented within the political system through a House of Chiefs.

This trend continued into the 1960s. At the turn of the decade, the government held a referendum that made the country a republic and also transformed Nkrumah from prime minister to president, removing some of the remaining checks on his authority. More far-reaching change came four years later, when the CPP used a second referendum to ban opposition parties and further increase the powers of the president. The political and economic failings of the ruling party saw its support base dwindle, and against a backdrop of mounting public dissatisfaction a **coup** removed Nkrumah from power in 1966, paving the way for three years of military rule under the National Liberation Council (NLC).

While some aspects of Ghana's story are unique, its general features were repeated in many other countries during this time period. Most independent African **states** did not start out life as authoritarian regimes. Instead, the constitutions established at the end of the colonial era typically sought to enshrine basic democratic values, and almost all recognized the principle of "one person one vote," gave full political rights to women, and established checks and balances of one form or another. These included a directly elected legislature, as well as a written constitution protected by a judiciary that was officially independent from the ruling party.

However, as in Ghana, these political systems rarely lasted long. Indeed, many countries did not even enjoy an initial, more optimistic period in which they appeared to be on course to consolidate a democratic political framework, as Ghana did. Instead, states such as the Republic of Congo (later Democratic Republic of Congo) and Togo suffered coups or civil conflict within just a few years of gaining independence. In other words, it was not so much that democracy broke down but that it was never established in the first place. Why did so many African states become authoritarian regimes so quickly? We will explore this question over the next three chapters, but part of the answer is that colonial rule predisposed African states toward more centralized and repressive forms of government.

While European powers typically encouraged formally democratic constitutions to be adopted during the negotiations that brought about independence, they had done little to create the conditions within which democratic politics could thrive. There were two key elements to this. First, the colonial era was characterized by systematic attempts to deny Africans their political and economic rights and stymie the emergence of popular nationalist parties. This typically involved highly repressive legislation that enabled governments to censor the media, ban public meetings, and detain political leaders on flimsy charges. All of these policies were enacted by states that were extremely centralized and in which the colonial governor wielded vast power.

In addition to the continent's authoritarian inheritance, a second important factor that complicated the prospects for democratization was the social consequences of colonialism. Managing vast territories with small numbers of officials ensured that colonial rule could not be sustained through coercion alone. It was therefore essential for colonial powers to find ways to co-opt support from African leaders and communities, which in turn meant that in many countries colonial governments actively invested in strengthening the positions of individuals who were willing to cooperate. The emergence of powerful "big men" during this period played an important role in shaping the way that African leaders have had to operate ever since.

Given this colonial legacy, Africa's democratic moment at the start of the 1960s is best thought of as a short-lived episode that – with the exception of a small number of states such as Botswana and Mauritius – interrupted two longer periods of authoritarian rule. It was short-lived precisely because it rested on such shaky foundations.

However, while these historical continuities created barriers to democratization, other features of colonial rule also complicated the ability of African leaders to retain power. Because colonial states typically built only the infrastructure needed to retain control over the capital city and the key trade routes required to export goods and resources, African leaders inherited political systems that were poorly placed to maintain a grip over rural areas and to police their own borders. As a result, military regimes and one-party states have often struggled to contain dissent and eradicate opposition, leading to a form of government that we call *fragile authoritarianism.*

## THE COLONIAL LEGACY

With one or two rare exceptions, the political systems that colonial powers constructed were designed to extract economic resources for the lowest possible cost. Early colonial states were typically built around ports—because this is where Europeans first landed and because they played a critical role in the import and export of goods—and well-located cities where the climate was more congenial. From this base, a small number of roads and railways were then established to connect these areas to the parts of the country where natural resources and agricultural production were located. This helps to explain why so many African capital cities are located on the coast (Map 1.1).

The end of World War II led to a period of investment in public services and infrastructure by colonial powers. This was partly a response to the growth of nationalist movements—which were often spurred on by the return of African soldiers demanding greater recognition of the important role that they had played in fighting on the side of the Allied forces against fascism. Expenditure on services also increased because the postwar period saw growing international

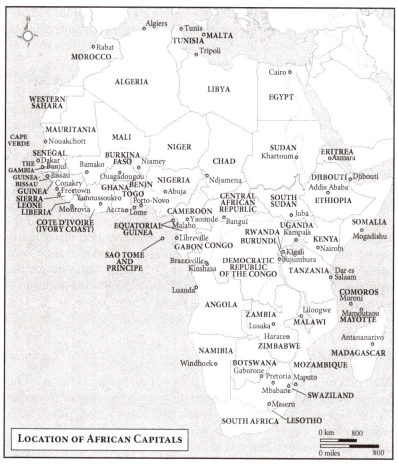

**MAP 1.1**    Location of African capital cities, 2016
*Source*: Lizard Point 2018.

pressure from organizations such as the United Nations to justify colonial rule, and providing development was one way to do this. However, although considerably more was spent on providing education and healthcare during this period, it remained wholly insufficient, and little was done to prepare countries and societies for independence.

On the one hand, investment in education was so limited and late that many countries entered independence with only a small number of university graduates and a relatively small pool of experienced administrators. For example, Zambia is said to have come to independence with only a hundred university graduates. In turn, this made the task of **Africanization**—replacing colonial personnel with African officials and transforming, or replacing, colonial state institutions—significantly more difficult, and in many countries colonial officials stayed on at the request of the new, post-independence governments.

At the same time, domestic political elites were given little exposure to democratic forms of government. Locked out of political power for much of the colonial era, the election of African representatives to the legislature was only achieved after many years of struggle. Moreover, in most cases the right to vote itself was only extended to all adult citizens during the 1950s and 1960s—with the franchise being limited in some cases to men until the mid-1960s. There were a few exceptions to this general rule. In Senegal, the French colonial regime extended citizenship rights to the inhabitants of the Four Communes (the oldest four colonial towns) in 1848, and in 1916 an African was elected to the French National Assembly in Paris for the first time. Competitive legislative elections to the government of Senegal also began comparatively early, with key figures such as Léopold Sédar Senghor—the future president—elected in 1951, nine years before independence. However, the Senegalese experience was rare. More often than not, African leaders took power just before or at independence and so had little experience of managing a large state.

On the other hand, the institutional inheritance of most African countries predisposed them toward a form of authoritarian rule. While colonial governments relied on co-opting local leaders to maintain control, this was underpinned by the use of force. It is true that in a small number of countries, such as Zambia, initial colonial conquest occurred more through the signing of treaties with African rulers than the prosecution of military campaigns. But in many cases, African resistance was put down by colonial armies with considerable loss of life—a period that John Londsale (1989) has referred to as the "conquest state."

The maintenance of foreign political domination also included considerable repression, especially in settler states (Box 1.3). Anticolonial campaigners were often detained without trial, found guilty in court proceedings that were anything but fair, and subjected to long periods of imprisonment and in some cases hanged, as research by David M. Anderson (2005) on colonial Kenya has demonstrated. Sustaining this

## Box 1.3   Settler Colonialism

Colonial governments tended to invest in the development of stronger states in territories that featured a higher number of European settlers. These were people of European descent who were encouraged by their governments to move to Africa in order to run businesses and farms, with the promise that they would be given privileged access to economic opportunities. For the colonial powers, this served two purposes. First, racist assumptions about skills and knowledge meant that they assumed (usually incorrectly) that their own citizens would do a better job of developing African economies. Second, emigration to Africa helped to reduce the problem of unemployment back home.

Where large settler populations developed, as in Angola (173,000 by the 1960s), Kenya (67,000), Mozambique (200,000), Namibia (68,000), and Zimbabwe (270,000), their presence changed the nature of colonial rule in a number of important respects. Settler groups were often effective at pushing colonial governments to introduce policies in their favor, which typically resulted in greater efforts to take land away from Africans and to develop services for the benefit of European communities. Moreover, European governments often fought hardest to prevent decolonization in these states because they wanted to protect the interests of the settler groups that they had persuaded to relocate to Africa in the first place.

One consequence of these developments was that colonial governments in countries such as Kenya constructed more effective state infrastructures, for example by employing more officials and expanding the security forces. Taken together with the refusal of European governments to meet the demands of African nationalists, this ensured that the struggle for independence in places like Angola, Mozambique, and Zimbabwe was particularly conflictual and drawn out—introducing a more violent form of politics, the legacy of which is still felt today.

system required the construction of a legal framework that facilitated the abuse of power. Thus, colonial governments were established as authoritarian regimes with few checks and balances on the powers of the governor and sweeping powers to control the lives of African "subjects" (Mamdani 1996). Even when elements of democracy were introduced later on, these were typically manipulated to suit colonial needs. For example, in both Kenya and Nigeria, colonial governments attempted—not always successfully—to influence elections by manipulating the rules on who could stand and who could vote to boost the chances of UK-friendly parties, and hence protect Britain's privileged relationship into the independence era (Cheeseman 2015: 147).

It should therefore be clear that if colonial government taught the aspiring African political elite anything it was how to use a combination of co-optation and coercion to demobilize popular movements. Indeed, when postcolonial African governments have restricted the basic freedoms of their citizens, such as speech, movement, and association, they have often done so by using colonial-era legislation that has yet to be removed from the statute books.

## BIG-MAN POLITICS

The construction of colonial political systems also transformed African politics in another important respect. In the 1800s, there were relatively few European-style states on the continent. It is true that the Kingdom of Ashanti developed a powerful trading network and sophisticated political system in the 1870s, which collected a form of taxation and had fearsome warriors at its disposal. Other areas with more centralized authority included the Lozi Kingdom in what is now Zambia and the Zulu Kingdom in southern Africa. The Sokoto Caliphate also developed a complex system of administration that linked thirty different Islamic emirates and over ten million people in West Africa. But these were exceptions rather than the rule. In 1850, centralized systems of political authority only covered around 10 percent of the continent.

Instead, people tended to live in smaller groupings. In some cases, it is clear that African societies did not recognize a strong central authority figure at all. For example, Igbo communities in what is now South-East Nigeria lived in relatively small villages and did not have a "king" or chief who could exert authority over the entire ethnic group. In communities like this, decisions by traditional leaders were expected to be made in consultation with the wider population. In turn, this placed limits on the extent to which power could be abused—although it is important to note that this does not necessarily mean that these political systems should be thought of as democracies. Bill Freund (2016) has argued that many of these groups were highly unequal and that public meetings were often dominated by older, wealthier, men.

They were, though, a long way from being centralized political systems capable of mass repression. Colonial rule fundamentally changed this picture in two ways. First, colonial regimes did not have enough officials to run their territories, and so they looked for existing leaders and power structures that they could collaborate with in order to maintain political stability (see Box 1.4). In many cases, this involved providing willing collaborators with funding and military support. In return, traditional leaders were expected to manage their communities and prevent a rebellion against colonial rule.

---

### Box 1.4   Colonial Variations: Belgian, British, French, and Portuguese Rule in Africa

Colonial regimes shared certain similarities. They were all economically exploitative, involved considerable repression, and were based on racist assumptions about the natural superiority of white Europeans. However, they also varied in terms of how they thought about African citizens and the kinds of governments that they established.

French rule in what is now Benin, Cameroon, Chad, Senegal, and Togo was distinctive in its stated commitment to "assimilation." This was the idea that African "natives" could be considered French—and hence entitled to the same rights as French citizens—if they adopted the French language, culture, and customs. The most complete realization of the idea of assimilation in Africa came in the Four Communes (colonial towns) of Senegal. In 1848, in the midst of the French Revolution, residents of the Four Communes were given voting rights and allowed to elect a **Deputy** to the Assembly in Paris. However, in reality the rhetoric of assimilation was rarely sustained in practice; even in Senegal the rights afforded to the *originaires* who had learned the French language and customs in the Four Communes were not extended to those in rural areas.

British rule in places like Ghana, Kenya, Nigeria, and Zambia had no such pretensions toward assimilation and instead focused on working with existing social and leadership structures. As a result, it is most associated with the policy of "indirect rule." This was a system through which the government relied on the co-optation of intermediaries—traditional leaders, ethnic big men, and so on—to maintain order and stability in the absence of the workforce and resources required to establish a more direct system of administration. The most famous version of this system was implemented in Nigeria by Frederick Lugard, who believed that it was the only way to manage a vast territory with only a small number of British officials. However, while this system of governance is often associated with British colonial rule, in reality most colonial regimes featured elements of indirect rule, while the British adopted a more direct model in settler colonies such as Kenya.

The Portuguese empire in Africa was smaller, encompassing what are now six countries, but was particularly drawn out and had an especially violent end. Portugal refused to agree to decolonization in part because its trade with its colonies—most notably Angola and Mozambique—was so important to the country's economy, and to Portuguese influence around the world. This led to prolonged wars of liberation that only came to an end with the Carnation Revolution of 1974 in Portugal, which overthrew the old colonial government and led to far-reaching political change both at home and abroad.

Belgian colonial rule was also particularly brutal. King Leopold, the second king of Belgium from 1865 to 1909, effectively owned what is now the Democratic Republic of Congo as a private individual and committed a vast range of human rights abuses including a system of forced labor in his drive to export minerals, rubber, and ivory from the country. In 1908, a public outcry led to control over the Congo passing out of Leopold's hands to the Belgium civil administration, but thereafter this the system of government continued to be highly authoritarian. However, it is important to remember that while Belgian colonialism has a particularly bad reputation, British and French administrations also committed a number of atrocities both in establishing colonial rule and defending it against the challenge of African nationalism.

Because it benefitted colonial governments to engage with a smaller number of leaders who could deliver the support of a greater number of people, and because colonial officials falsely assumed that all Africans lived in hierarchically ordered "tribes", this process transferred greater power into the hands of a smaller number of people. In some cases—such as among Igbo communities in southeastern Nigeria—this actually involved *creating* powerful chiefs where they had not previously existed. For their part, many African communities rejected the imposition of leaders whom they saw to be illegitimate, leading to fierce protests and the evolution of anticolonial movements (see Box 1.5). However, others saw that the best way to secure political and economic opportunities under European rule was to comply with colonial assumptions, and they quickly adapted to the rules of the new political game. As a result of the work of such "cultural entrepreneurs"

---

### Box 1.5 African Responses to Colonial Rule

*There were many different African responses to colonial rule, but one of the best known is the Négritude movement that was pioneered by Léopold Senghor, an author and future Senegalese president, and Aimé Césaire, a poet and political leader from Martinique. Senghor describes Négritude as a movement that initially evolved out of African poetry – an example of which can be found below – and popular culture, and then developed into a political philosophy that emphasized the importance of African values and explicitly rejected European values and assumptions. Later, the horrors of the 1930s and 1940s, and in particular the way in which racial hatred drove mass killings and the Holocaust by Nazi Germany, led the movement to evolve in a more inclusive way that placed greater emphasis on the way that Africans could benefit from engaging in a conversation with ideas from other cultures. Some of the ideas within Négritude have had an enduring legacy. Most significantly, Sénghor's emphasis on the "community mindedness" of black peoples has underpinned the argument that consensus may be more "African" than electoral competition—an idea we return to in Chapter 5.*

My négritude is not a stone, its deafness rush against the clamor of the day
My blackness is not a pillow of water, rush against the clamor of the day
My négritude is not a dead water cover, on the dead eye of the earth
My négritude is neither a tower nor a cathedral
She dives into the red flesh of the soil
She plunges into the fiery flesh of the sky
She pierces the opaque dejection of her right patience.

Aimé Césaire (1973)

In as much as the word *latinité* (Latinity in English) expresses a concept which defines the qualities of Latin civilization, the work *negritude* expresses the same for the whole range of values of civilization of all black peoples in the world . . .

. . . In the field of politics, I shall point out the pattern of community mindedness. In the traditional negro-African world, the society was made up on concentric communities scaled up one over the other, from the family cell to the kingdom and in which various socio-professional groups were linked up with each other by a system of reciprocal integration.

Léopold Senghor (1974)

(Vail 1989), ethnic groups such as the Kikuyu in Kenya quickly began to campaign for the colonial government to recognize a "paramount chief" to represent their community in the hope that this would ensure that their needs and interests would be more effectively represented.

In this way, colonial rule, and the response to it by African communities, helped to create *big men*—powerful figures capable of exerting great authority over large ethnic groups. The term "big men" is a useful metaphor because these leaders were "big" in the sense that they could wield vast power, and also in the sense that they were very wealthy and consumed large amounts of food, becoming "big" in terms of the shape of their bodies.

The fact that these individuals were almost always men is also important. In addition to racist stereotypes about how Africans lived, Europeans imported sexist stereotypes regarding the appropriate role of women and men in a society (Bush 2014). This meant that colonial political and economic policies disadvantaged women. In some cases, women had also been marginalized before colonial rule. But in a number of African societies, women had historically played an important role in valuable economic activities, and could exert significant influence when it came to making decisions within the family and the community. A small number of ethnic groups also featured female traditional leaders. European intervention undermined many of these practices, ensuring that more gender-balanced societies did not emerge.

Thus, colonialism laid the foundations for African politics to become dominated by a competition between rival community leaders, and by men.

The second important change triggered by colonial rule was the creation of geographically large states, which made it possible for "big men" to wield much greater power—and commit much greater abuses—than was previously possible. Whereas only a small proportion of the continent featured centralized kingdoms in the 1800s, and the power of most leaders was limited by the capacity of their followers to migrate out of their sphere of authority if they were too abusive (Herbst 1990), by the 1960s Africa had been divided into a set of distinct territories almost all of which featured a central government including a bureaucracy and security forces. Consequently, in many countries postcolonial presidents enjoyed the potential to wield power over a diverse group of communities for the first time. However, in practice their capacity to do so was limited, first by the underdeveloped nature of the states that they inherited, and second by the presence of rival big men seeking to contest their hold on power. In turn, this complicated colonial legacy lay the foundations for the politics of fragile authoritarianism that would characterize the experience of many African countries over the next eighty years.

The colonial period also gave rise to another significant tension after independence. Because the authority of the big men that emerged was rooted in their position as leaders of a specific ethnic or linguistic group, those who won national office often felt obliged to look after the needs of their own community first, even though they were officially supposed to rule in the interests of all. This tension had a number of important consequences. One was that presidents from one ethnic group tended to exclude people from rival communities from access to government resources. Such "winner-takes-all" or "zero-sum" politics, in which only the supporters of the president benefit while he is in office, was hugely damaging. Most obviously, it encouraged different ethnic groups and their leaders to compete for power—and to fear that they would suffer a lower standard of living if they were not successful. In many cases, this competition became so heated that it harmed the relationship between different communities, and in some cases led to political violence and civil war, as we will see in Chapter 3.

These issues were compounded by the fact that the colonial powers had drawn the borders of virtually all newly independent African states with little regard for the reality on the ground, often slicing through precolonial societies, communities, and polities. European governments had scant interest in ensuring that their African colonies were built around existing, coherent political entities and focused instead on carving up the continent's peoples and resources among them. This occurred most notoriously during the 1884–1885

Berlin Conference, when some of the delegates simply drew straight lines on a map to delineate new colonial territories. The artificiality of these boundaries to those who lived near and across them is demonstrated by the fact that two brothers born during the colonial era in the borderlands between Kenya and Uganda would later become senior politicians in separate countries, with Moody Awori serving as vice president of Kenya from 2003 to 2008 and Aggrey Awori as a Ugandan Cabinet minister from 2009 to 2011.

Most post-independence African rulers were therefore faced with the challenge of governing and unifying collections of communities that had no real sense of being part of a common nation-state. Chief Obafemi Awolowo, later the penultimate premier of colonial Western Nigeria, wrote in 1947 that "Nigeria is not a nation, it is a mere geographical expression" (Awolowo 1947). For many post-independence leaders faced with this colonial inheritance, mobilizing support around their own ethnic group rather than a putative nation represented not only good politics but also, seemingly, a necessity.

A final important legacy of colonialism was that the democratic institutions that were created to govern independent African states were often undermined from within because the leaders who took power had little experience of democratic government and found it relatively easy to break or change laws that were supposed to prevent them from abusing their power. We will explore the nature and impact of this development in more depth in later chapters, but for now it is important to note that the fusion of societies in which big men were empowered to wield great authority with European political systems in which individual power was supposed to be limited by institutional checks and balances led to the emergence of a type of politics that is often called **neo-patrimonialism**. A key feature of neo-patrimonial systems is that leaders are often able to use their personal authority, family ties, ethnic identity, and the distribution of gifts (**patrimonialism**) to break the rules or amend them in their favor. As a result, the institutions of the state, such as legislatures and judiciaries, did not work as they were supposed to on paper.

It is important not to exaggerate the extent to which Africa is "neo-patrimonial". In reality, there is considerable variation in the power of individual leaders and the strength of formal political institutions, as we shall see in Chapters Three and Five. Nonetheless, the cumulative impact of colonial rule was extremely problematic. The authoritarian aspects of African societies were intensified, while the more inclusive and democratic elements were undermined.

## CONCLUSION: UNDERSTANDING FRAGILE AUTHORITARIANISM

The complex and uneven impact of colonial rule set many African states on a pathway toward fragile authoritarianism. On the one hand, this era laid the foundations for the undermining of democratic constitutions immediately after independence. On the other, it also generated major challenges for the continent's authoritarian leaders.

Colonial states were characterized by a center-periphery divide in that they could exert great control over the "center" (the capital city and its environs) but often had much weaker control when it came to the "periphery" (far-flung rural areas in which there would typically only be a very small number of colonial officials, and in some cases, none at all) (Herbst 2014). Colonial governments often responded to this challenge by substituting for the lack of an extensive state machinery by co-opting big men, who it relied on to deliver the support, or at least acquiescence of their communities.

After independence, most African governments lacked the resources needed to make up for this deficit. While there was a great rush to engage in state-building activities and to develop an infrastructure that would enable the ruling party to deliver services and exert political control, more often than not these efforts stalled before they got going. In a context of limited resources and a prolonged period of economic decline that began to take hold in the early 1970s, the majority of leaders chose to focus on solving short-term problems such as staying in power, rather than investing in the long-term job of enhancing **state capacity**.

As a result, constructing totalitarian regimes—in which the state uses repression and control over information to regulate all aspects of life—was often all but impossible. Some governments did emerge that sought to exert this degree of authority with considerable success, such as the apartheid regime in South Africa and, much later, Paul Kagame's Rwanda (see Chapter 5). But for the most part, leaders quickly recognized that the size of the security forces was too small, and their countries too large, for this to be the sole source of their authority.

In this sense, postcolonial states reproduced a core feature of colonial rule: although they could deal very effectively and brutally with sporadic challenges to their authority, they were poorly placed to withstand a broader uprising. This type of government is best thought of as a form of fragile authoritarianism, in which the outward appearance of total domination does not match the internal reality of underdeveloped states and vulnerable leaders. One consequence of this particular colonial inheritance was that the most stable authoritarian regimes were not necessarily the ones that used the most violence, but the ones that managed to find an effective balance between coercion and co-optation. As in the colonial era, political stability was rarely achieved through repression alone; instead, it depended on the ability of leaders to cultivate the support of certain groups and big men.

This is one reason that the state of the economy and the ideas used by the government to justify its actions proved to be so important—as we shall see in the next two chapters.

## REFERENCES

Anderson, David M. *Histories of the Hanged: Britain's Dirty War in Kenya and the End of Empire: Testimonies from the Mau Mau Rebellion in Kenya.* New York: W. W. Norton, 2005.

Awolowo, Obafemi. *Path to Nigerian Freedom.* London: Faber and Faber, 1947.

Bush, Barbara. "Motherhood, Morality, and Social Order: Gender and Development Discourse and Practice in Late Colonial Africa." In *Developing Africa: Concepts and Practices in Twentieth-Century Colonialism*, edited by Joseph M. Hodge, Gerald Hödl, and Martina Kopf, 270–93. Manchester, UK: Manchester University Press, 2014.

Cheeseman, Nic. *Democracy in Africa: Successes, Failures, and the Struggle for Political Reform.* Cambridge: Cambridge University Press, 2015.

Freund, Bill. *The Making of Contemporary Africa: The Development of African Society Since 1800.* Basingstoke, UK: Palgrave Macmillan, 2016.

Herbst, Jeffrey. "Migration, the Politics of Protest, and State Consolidation in Africa." *African Affairs* 89, no. 355 (1990): 183–203.

Herbst, Jeffrey. *States and Power in Africa.* Princeton, NJ: Princeton University Press, 2014.

Mamdani, Mahmood. *Citizen and Subject: Contemporary Africa and the Legacy of Late Colonialism.* Princeton, NJ: Princeton University Press, 1996.

Ranger, Terence. "The Invention of Tradition in Colonial Africa." In *The Invention of Tradition*, edited by Eric Hobsbawm and Terence Ranger, 211–62. Cambridge: Cambridge University Press, 1983.

Senghor, Léopold Sédar. "Négritude." *Indian Literature* 17, no. 1/2 (1974): 269–73.

Vail, Leroy, ed. *The Creation of Tribalism in Southern Africa.* Berkeley, CA: University of California Press, 1989.

## SUGGESTED READINGS

Achebe, Chinua. *Things Fall Apart*. Portsmouth, NH: Heinemann Educational Books Ltd, 1958.

Bob-Milliar, George M. "Chieftaincy, Diaspora, and Development: The Institution of Nksuohene in Ghana." *African Affairs* 108, no. 433 (2009): 541–58.

Boone, Catherine. *Merchant Capital and the Roots of State Power in Senegal, 1930–1985*. Cambridge: Cambridge University Press, 1992.

Cabral, Amilcar. *Unity and Struggle: Speeches and Writings*. New York, NY: Monthly Review Press, 1979.

Cooper, Fred. *Africa Since 1940: The Past of the Present*. Cambridge: Cambridge University Press, 2002.

Diop, Cheikh Anta. *The African Origin of Civilisation: Myth or Reality*. Chicago: Chicago Review Press, 1989.

Ekeh, Peter P. "Colonialism and the Two Publics in Africa: A Theoretical Statement." *Comparative Studies in Society and History* 17, no. 1 (1975): 91–112.

Elkins, Caroline. *Britain's Gulag: The Brutal End of Empire in Kenya*. London: Pimlico, 2005.

Erdmann, Gero, and Ulf Engel. "Neopatrimonialism Reconsidered: Critical Review and Elaboration of an Elusive Concept." *Commonwealth & Comparative Politics* 45, no. 1 (2007): 95–119.

Horton, Robin. "Stateless Societies in the History of West Africa." *History of West Africa* 1, (1971): 78–119.

Lonsdale, John. "The Cconquest Sstate, 1895–1904.," Iin William Ochieng, ed., *A Modern History oOf Kenya*, 6–35. Nairobi: Evans Brothers, 1989: 6–35.

Lugard, Frederick J. D. *The Dual Mandate in British Tropical Africa*. London: Routledge, 2013.

Mainga, Mutumba. *Bulozi under the Luyana Kings: Political Evolution and State Formation in Pre-Colonial Zambia*. London: Longman, 1973.

Mazrui, Ali Al'Amin. *Power, Politics, and the African Condition*. Trenton, NJ: Africa World Press, 2004.

McCaskie, Tom. C. *State and Society in Pre-Colonial Asante*. Cambridge: Cambridge University Press, 2003.

Newbury, Catharine. *The Cohesion of Oppression: Clientship and Ethnicity in Rwanda, 1860–1960*. New York: Columbia University Press, 1989.

# Between Tradition and Modernity

## *Identity, Ideas, and the Building of the Authoritarian African State, 1965–85*

Ethiopia's long line of emperors officially came to an end in March 1975, when the thousand-year-old Abyssinian monarchy was formally abolished. Haile Selassie I—who descended, according to court genealogists, from King Solomon and the Queen of Sheba, and whose many titles included "Elect of God"—had been deposed the previous September by a Marxist-Leninist military *junta* known as the *Derg* ("committee" in Amharic, the language of Ethiopia's then ruling elite). The incoming regime had appointed Haile Selassie's son, Amha Selassie, as emperor-designate in his father's place but soon reversed its position, annulling this decision and the imperial system with it in a proclamation issued on March 21.

For the new, socialist regime, the imperial tradition had sustained and celebrated an unjust, anachronistic, **feudal system** of government, which rested on the abuse and exploitation of the peasantry. The *Derg*'s eventual leader, Colonel Mengistu Hailemariam, set about energetically implementing a radical program of land reform, later justifying his policies by explaining the importance of replacing the "very backward, archaic, and feudalist system" of the empire. The impression he wished to present was that of a clean break with the past—a fundamental shift from absolute monarchy to revolutionary socialism. This drastic transition left little room for sentiment or nostalgia in dealing with Haile Selassie; Ethiopia's purported 225th emperor died a prisoner in August 1975, his body hurriedly buried beneath a latrine in the grounds of Addis Ababa's Menelik Palace.

Over time, however, the public image cultivated by Mengistu became increasingly blurred with that of his imperial predecessors. He moved into Haile Selassie's former palace, retaining its suite of servants and vehicles, and sat on the throne of past emperors to watch parades and receive visitors. He frequently compared himself to reformist nineteenth-century emperor Tewodros II and insisted, according to deputy foreign minister Dawit Wolde Giorgis (1989), that he be addressed by the formal Amharic word for "you," as emperors had been before. Addis Ababa–based artists began to depict Mengistu as the semidivine mediator between heaven and earth, as they had done for Haile Selassie—albeit replacing the Father, Son, and Holy Ghost in their murals with **Karl Marx, Friedrich Engels, and Vladimir Lenin** (Clapham 1988: 79). Gossip was even spread at court about Mengistu's own imperial ancestry; his mother was supposedly the illegitimate daughter of a nobleman who himself was the illegitimate son of the revered, conquering emperor Menelik II. "He had become," according to Dawit, "the new emperor."

To some extent, Mengistu's self-exaltation was the result of what Dawit describes as the dictator's long-standing "insatiable thirst for power"; "absolute power," as Lord Acton observed in 1887, "corrupts absolutely." But there is more to it than this. Authoritarian rulers, as we have already found, can rarely remain in office through force alone. This has been particularly true for postcolonial Africa, as the last chapter explained, where the formal reach of the state has frequently been very limited outside of large towns and cities (though Ethiopia, of course, was one of only two African states not to be colonized). What has often helped to sustain African authoritarianism has been the ability of regimes to conform with popular understandings of what legitimate public authority *is*—a government doing what a government should do, and looking like what a government should look like.

In 1970s Ethiopia, to the mind of Mengistu, most people had only ever known government by emperors, whose right to rule had been based around ideas on heredity, deference, military strength, and divine election. Elsewhere on the continent, as this chapter shows,

African leaders identified other ideas and authorities as central. In many cases, supposed precolonial traditions such as **chieftaincy**, kingship and community decision making would be claimed by, and embedded within, emerging authoritarian systems. They therefore reappeared in the concepts used by those in power to legitimate their rule in the postcolonial era, such as *ujamaa* (Swahili for "extended family") in Tanzania and *retour à l'authenticité* ("return to authenticity" in French) in Zaire. Importantly, many of these ideas stood in opposition to standard understandings of multiparty democracy.

As the previous chapter outlined, the kinds of institutions that African leaders took charge of at independence—armies, police forces, national assemblies, political parties and trade unions to name the most common—had limited parallels in the precolonial period. Many authoritarian leaders therefore recognized that they needed to imbue these new instruments of political power with traditional, or pseudotraditional, ideas about authority in order to build and maintain popular support. This was particularly important given the vast territories many post-independence African governments had to try and govern. In this context, tapping into deep rooted ideas about authority that resonated with the citizenry represented an important way to "broadcast state power"—to use Jeffrey Herbst's evocative term (2014).

This is not to say, of course, that these ideas have always enjoyed widespread acceptance among African peoples—far from it. Nor is it to suggest that violence and coercion have not been integral and deeply problematic facets of authoritarian rule across the continent. In Mengistu's Ethiopia, for example, his *Derg* regime presided over a brutal crackdown of perceived opponents and "reactionaries" during 1977–1978. The *Qey Shibir*—or "Ethiopian Red Terror"—saw hundreds of thousands captured, killed, or executed, including journalists, pregnant women, worshippers at church services, and children. This chapter nonetheless argues that coercion, and co-option, cannot *fully* explain the durability and resilience of authoritarian forms of government in Africa: ideas also matter.

## AUTHORITARIAN TYPOLOGIES IN THE POSTINDEPENDENCE ERA

During the 1970s, a number of different types of political system emerged across Africa. In a small number of cases (Table 2.1), decolonization did not occur and instead a form of European or white

**TABLE 2.1**    Range of Political Regimes in Africa in the 1970s, Selected
Examples

| One-Party Rule | Military Regime | Personal Rule | Multiparty Democracy | White-Minority Rule |
|---|---|---|---|---|
| Benin | Ethiopia | DRC* | Botswana | Namibia |
| Kenya | Ghana | Malawi | Gambia | South Africa |
| Senegal | Nigeria | | Mauritius | Zimbabwe** |
| Tanzania | Togo | | | |
| Zambia | Uganda | | | |

*Then called Zaïre.
**Then called Rhodesia.

minority rule continued. The latter outcome occurred where control of
the government passed from colonial powers into the hands of white
leaders from the European settler communities that had been encouraged to emigrate to places like Namibia and Zimbabwe. When these
white governments refused to give up power, both rejecting the claims
of African nationalists and asserting their independence from colonial
rule, the result was white minority governments that ruled over black
majority populations through force.

This reached its extreme in South Africa, where the National
Party elected in 1948 pursued a policy of racial segregation and subju-
gation that was known as *apartheid* (separateness). Under this system,
laws were passed that determined where nonwhites could go, where
they could live, whom they could marry, and what jobs they could do.
Apartheid rule was backed up by the use of systematic repression,
implemented by one of the continent's largest and best-resourced
security forces. It was also underpinned by an unfair system of political representation in which only whites were given full political rights
and allowed to vote in national elections. Sustaining this system in the
face of mass opposition required the government to use brutal force,
including a number of atrocities such as the 1960 Sharpeville massacre in which sixty-nine people died after police fired on protestors
who were campaigning against laws that restricted their movement.
Among the dead and injured were dozens of children.

A more common form of political system was the one-party state,
in which the ruling party steadily extended its control over the political system until the point at which no other parties were allowed to
exist. These systems often had greater legitimacy than other forms of

authoritarian government because they were typically established by nationalist parties that had won convincing victories in elections held in the late colonial and early independence period. Moreover, many of these states allowed "fragments of democracy" to remain, in that they permitted citizens to elect their representatives to parliament through regular polls (Cheeseman 2015). In this way, they blurred the line between authoritarian and democratic politics. Although people could not choose the ruling party, and could not determine its policies, it was sometimes possible for civil society groups such as trade unions to push for changes that would benefit their members—as we will see in the next chapter. It was also possible to unseat government ministers—even if their opponents were from the same party and voting against the president himself (or, in rare cases, herself—see Box 2.1) was impossible.

### Box 2.1   Women Leaders in Authoritarian Africa

There have been a small number of short-lived periods of female leadership in authoritarian African states, though none have lasted longer than fifteen months—with the exception of Mozambique's Luísa Diogo, who served as that country's prime minister between 2004 and 2010. In most cases, the women in question have been appointed prime minister by authoritarian—male—presidents or have become acting president in a caretaker capacity. Their political influence, perhaps paradoxically, has generally been most acute *prior* to their elevation to the premiership or presidency, when they were government ministers, advisers, or legislators.

Elisabeth Domitien, for example, played an important role in Central African Republic (CAR)'s independence movement as head of its women's group. After independence, she served as an adviser to president David Dacko and vice president of the ruling party. She was appointed prime minister by the man who overthrew Dacko, army chief Jean-Bédel Bokassa, in January 1975 in part to enhance his international reputation (1975 was declared International Women's Year by the United Nations). Domitien was, however, dismissed by the increasingly tyrannical Bokassa fifteen months later when she refused to support his bid to elevate himself to the title of emperor.

Elsewhere on the continent, Carmen Pereira, president of Guinea-Bissau's National Assembly, served as the country's acting president for two days in May 1984 while Sylvie Kinigi and Agathe

Uwilingiyimana were appointed prime ministers of Burundi and Rwanda, respectively, in July 1993, leaving office (and, in Uwilingiyimana's case, murdered) less than a year later.

Ruth Perry was briefly appointed acting head of state of Liberia by the regional organization the Economic Community of West African States (ECOWAS) in September 1996. Perry had originally become involved in Liberian politics through her husband, judge and lawmaker McDonald Perry, but became a senator in 1985 after his death. Her involvement in civil society groups and women's movements during Liberia's 1989–1997 civil war marked her out as a force for unity in the postwar era, hence her appointment by ECOWAS.

Being perceived as a neutral, unifying figure also led to the appointment of Catherine Samba-Panza as acting president of the Central African Republic in January 2014 following that country's 2013–2014 civil conflict. Samba-Panza had previously been a respected businessperson and Mayor of Bangui (CAR's capital) and was elected to the post by members of parliament after assuring them of her impartiality. As acting president, Samba-Panza was barred from standing in CAR's 2015–2016 election, and her term ended in March 2016.

These aspects of one-party rule were important to the way in which governments sought to legitimize their political system, because leaders could claim that their regimes respected human rights. Indeed, the first Zambian President, Kenneth Kaunda, argued that his one-party state was more democratic than the multiparty systems in the United States and the United Kingdom, on the basis that while those systems only allowed citizens to vote once every four or five years, his government allowed them to constantly engage in the political process. Some of this was true—authoritarian systems such as those presided over by Kaunda, or Julius Nyerere in neighboring Tanzania, permitted various forms of political participation, including through trade union and party structures. In most cases, though, ordinary people found it extremely difficult to have their voices heard. Dissenters were arrested, and one-party states became increasingly authoritarian and violent when they began to lose popular support in the 1980s.

Despite this, most one-party states could still claim a better record on human rights than the personal dictatorships of Mobutu Seso Seko in Zaïre and Hastings Banda in Malawi. In these regimes, single individuals established themselves as the personal embodiment of government and constructed elaborate security mechanisms to protect their power. In Malawi, for example, President Banda employed seven different security agencies—most of which were tasked with monitoring and repressing his rivals, but some of which were used to spy on his allies and monitor what other agencies were doing in order to ensure that he would never be betrayed. At times, the personalized nature of Banda's authoritarianism verged on the absurd. The popular Simon and Garfunkel song "Cecilia"—released in 1970—was banned in Malawi for fear that it might offend the president and his powerful housekeeper and Official Hostess Cecilia Kadzamira.

Mobutu came to power through a coup, reflecting a broader trend. Between 1960 and 1975, thirty-five different leaders were overthrown as a result of military uprisings, leading to considerable political instability on the continent (see Box 2.2). Although the military often tried to justify its actions on the basis that it was "defending democracy from itself" and that the intervention was essential to maintain national unity and promote development, this rarely proved to be the case. Instead, the vast majority of governments in which military leaders sought to govern through the army—as opposed to trying to set up a system of personal rule or a one-party state—succumbed to many of the same faults that they had identified in civilian political systems: corruption, the abuse of power, and a failure to put the needs of the nation before their own self-interest.

## Box 2.2   Military Coups in Postcolonial Africa

From the 1960s to the 1970s, governments in a range of countries—including Ghana, Nigeria, and Mali—were overthrown in a military coup d'etat, which increasingly became the main way in which power changed hands, particularly in West and Central Africa.

As the following list shows, between 1960 and 1975, thirty-five African leaders were deposed by military officers in every region of the continent. Among those overthrown were some of Africa's leading nationalist icons, notably Congo's Patrice Lumumba, Ghana's Kwame Nkrumah, Uganda's Milton Obote, and Ethiopia's Haile Selassie, and this heralded an important shift away from civilian rule in much of Africa. Many coups were supported by former colonial states or Cold War superpowers—notably France, the United Kingdom, and the United States—who wished to see more politically pliable or ideologically aligned administrations installed. The close role the United Kingdom and France continued to play in training and supporting armies in their one-time colonies meant that they were particularly likely to be implicated in such activity.

Critically, though, coup leaders justified their actions—and right to govern—with reference to ideas and not just, or even primarily, their ability to neutralize opponents. In many cases, army chiefs presented the military as the reliable, patriotic embodiment of national unity, rescuing the country from the political chaos that had been created by squabbling, **sectarian** politicians. Military officers also represented their actions—which were often accompanied by the suspension of the constitution—as attempts to protect the rule of law and constitutional order from civilian leaders seeking to subvert them. This was, for example, the justification used by then Congolese army chief Joseph-Desiré Mobutu after his 1965 coup against President Joseph Kasa-Vubu. In other cases, such as the 1964 overthrow of Sultan Jamshib bin Abdulla Al Said of Zanzibar and the 1974 removal of Haile Selassie, these sentiments were mixed with Cold War language about opposing—or promoting—socialism.

Some of these ideas, particularly those around restoring stability and fostering unity, had widespread appeal across postcolonial African societies, many of which were divided along ethnic, religious, and cultural lines. Consequently, this language has continued to be used by coup leaders in Africa to the present day, even though coups themselves have become much less frequent since the 1990s. In announcing the November 2017 military removal of Zimbabwe's Robert Mugabe, for example, Major-General Sibusiso Moyo argued in a televised address that the army wished to "return our country to a dispensation that allows for investment, development, and prosperity" and to "pacify a degenerating political, social, and economic situation in our country which if not addressed may lead to violence."

*The following African leaders were removed through military coup between 1960 and 1975*:

*1960* (September 14): *Patrice Lumumba*, Prime Minister of the Republic of Congo (now Democratic Republic of Congo)

*1963* (January 13): *Sylvanus Olympio*, President of Togo

*1963* (August 15): *Fulbert Youlou*, President of the Republic of Congo

*1963* (October 28): *Hubert Maga*, President of Dahomey (now Benin)

*1964* (January 12): *Jamshid bin Abdullah Al Said*, Sultan of Zanzibar

*1964* (February 17): *Léon M'ba*, President of Gabon

*1965* (November 25): *Joseph Kasa-Vubu*, President of the Republic of Congo (now Democratic Republic of Congo)

*1965* (November 27): *Sourou-Migan Apithy*, President of Dahomey (now Benin)

*1966* (January 1): *David Dacko*, President of the Central African Republic

*1966* (January 3): *Maurice Yaméogo*, President of Upper Volta (now Burkina Faso)

*1966* (January 15): *Abubakar Tafawa Balewa*, Prime Minister of Nigeria

*1966* (February 4): *King Mutesa II of Buganda*, President of Uganda

*1966* (February 24): *Kwame Nkrumah*, President of Ghana

*1966* (July 8): *Mwambutsa IV*, King of Burundi

*1966* (July 29): *Johnson Aguiyi-Ironsi*, Head of State of Nigeria

*1966* (November 28): *Ntare V*, King of Burundi

*1967* (January 13): *Nicolas Grunitzky*, President of Togo

*1967* (March 21): *Siaka Stevens*, Prime Minister of Sierra Leone

*1967* (December 16): *Christophe Soglo*, President of Dahomey (now Benin)

*1968* (April 19): *Andrew Juxon-Smith*, Acting Governor-General of Sierra Leone

*1968* (September 4): *Alphonse Massamba-Débat*, President of the Republic of Congo

*1968* (November 19): *Modibo Keïta*, President of Mali

*1969* (May 25): *Ismail al-Azhari*, President of Sudan

*1969* (October 21): *Sheikh Mukhtar Mohamed Hussein*, President of Somalia

*1971* (January 25): *Milton Obote*, President of Uganda

*1972* (January 13): *Kofi Abrefa Busia*, Prime Minister of Ghana

*1972* (October 11): *Philibert Tsiranana*, President of Madagascar

*1972* (October 26): *Justin Ahomadégbé-Tomêtin*, Chairman of the Presidential Council of Dahomey (now Benin)

*1973* (July 5): *Grégoire Kayibanda*, President of Rwanda

*1974* (April 15): *Hamani Diori*, President of Niger

*1974* (September 12): *Haile Selassie I*, Emperor of Ethiopia

*1975* (February 5): *Gabriel Ramanantsoa*, President of Madagascar

*1975* (April 13): *François Tombalbaye*, President of Chad

*1975* (July 29): *Yakubu Gowon*, Head of State of Nigeria

*1975* (August 3): *Ahmed Abdallah Abderemane*, President of the Comoros

Military regimes also proved to be some of the most violent in the continent's history, in part because they had few avenues through which to assess public opinion. Military leaders often feared that they were not as popular as they claimed to be and as a result reacted with brutal force to any challenges to their authority. There was some reason for this fear. African leaders that left power during this period often found that life became very difficult: over 60 percent of those who left power were killed, prosecuted for the crimes they had committed, or forced into exile (Cheeseman and Klaas 2018). Military leaders knew this well, because in many cases they themselves had taken power through the barrel of a gun, often overthrowing a former ally—or, in the case of Teodoro Obiang Nguema Mbasogo of Equatorial Guinea, a close relative. Obiang Nguema ousted his own uncle, Francisco Macías Nguema, in an August 1979 coup and oversaw his trial and execution a few weeks later.

As a result, military rulers worried about the threat posed by potential rivals both outside and inside their own regimes. The consequences of this paranoia were often serious. In Nigeria, successive military governments stand accused of killing thousands of people during their time in power—in most cases without a trial, and in some cases through public executions. Many more were incarcerated, often on the basis of no evidence and without being told what the charges against them were or being allowed access to a lawyer.

Somewhat paradoxically, it is also true that extended military rule, and the sociopolitical upheaval it unleashed, at times opened up political and economic space for previously excluded groups. Alicia Decker's (2014) research on the lives of ordinary women in Idi Amin's Uganda, for example, details how the dictator's destructive policies resulted in more female-headed households as husbands and male relatives fled abroad. It also led to some economic advancement for women, whose labor was in much greater demand following Amin's 1972 expulsion of the Asian-Ugandan community from the country. Amin himself, however, increasingly came to promote a highly militarized and masculine idea of state and societal values which legitimized the policing of women's bodies (short skirts were banned in 1972) and the beating and raping of women by soldiers wishing to underscore their virility and unchecked authority. In summary, military leaders have rarely lived up to their promises.

While it is useful to have a sense of the different kinds of political systems that emerged in the 1970s, it is also important to note that this was a particularly fluid time. This makes classifying countries difficult, because many states went through a number of different systems in quick succession. For example, Ghana oscillated between military regimes and efforts to reintroduce civilian politics. The same was true of Uganda. In Benin, the military government that overthrew civilian rule set about forming a party and turned itself into a one-party state. Other political systems claimed to be a one-party state, but they did not really feature a meaningful party and are better thought as personal dictatorships. This is true of Malawi, which is why we have placed it under the category of "personal rule" in Table 2.1 above, when others might put it in a different category. The situation of Zaïre (now DRC) was more complicated still, because Mobutu came to power in a coup and later formed a political party to try and legitimate his rule, but he is generally classified as a personal dictator because army and party institutions made little difference to the way that he governed. Other countries spent long periods in conflict, during which time it was often hard to say what the system of government was, and indeed whether one really existed.

Keeping this fluidity in mind will be helpful when reading the rest of this book, because in the countries that we cover, African leaders and their people rarely felt that life was secure or predictable.

## THE POWER OF IDEAS

Regardless of regime type, in the 1960s and 1970s many authoritarian leaders sought to base the legitimacy of their rule in ideas, traditions, and concepts of government from African history—or, at least, an interpretation of that history. In some cases, including Jean-Bédel Bokassa regime in the Central African Republic's, these ideas were borrowed from the recently departed former colonial power. Bokassa, a military dictator who overthrew President David Dacko in 1966, declared himself "Emperor of Central Africa" in 1976. He established a short-lived, brutal "empire" built around narratives and iconography associated with France's one-time military leader-turned-emperor, Napoleon Bonaparte. Bokassa's lavish 1977 coronation was modeled on Napoleon's, with the new emperor riding in a carriage led by soldiers dressed in nineteenth-century French cavalry uniforms. Infamously, the ceremony cost the equivalent of Central African Republic's entire annual state budget.

### Unity

More often, though, authoritarian rulers turned to precolonial African history for their inspiration. In many cases, regimes presented to their parliaments and populations a version of this history where political

decisions had been made on the basis of consensus and—critically—
*unity*, rather than through competitive elections and partisan politics.
Julius Nyerere, who became Tanzania's first president in 1964, developed an entire ruling philosophy—*ujamaa*—around the idea of returning to a precolonial era of "traditional African democracy," where village
"elders sit under the big tree and talk until they agree" (Molony 2014:
126). The implementation of *ujamaa* in Tanzania involved the nation-
alization of key industries, the **collectivization of economic production** around village units and the fostering of national unity and identity
through free, compulsory education and the use of Swahili. To this day,
Tanzania is one of the only countries in Africa where a single, non-
European language is almost universally spoken and understood.

This idealized vision of a harmonious form of government posited
politics as a process which unified rather than divided communities,
an ideal that was often contrasted favorably with Western, multiparty
democratic systems, which Nyerere had once dismissed as "football
politics." Indeed, during the 1960s and 1970s, many authoritarian
African regimes came to depict **multiparty politics** as fundamentally
divisive and disruptive, and used this argument to legitimate creating
other kinds of political systems that they said would be better placed
to promote national unity. Most obviously, the one-party state—and
the prohibition of opposition parties that went with it—represented
the institutional embodiment of this appeal to unity. In Tanzania, the
Tanganyika African National Union (TANU) and its successor, Chama
Cha Mapinduzi, was the only legal party until 1992. As we have already seen, one-party states also emerged in a large number of other
countries, including Benin, Kenya, Senegal, and Zambia.

Over time, authoritarian leaders further expanded their critique
of the problems of multiparty democracy, which was often depicted as
being intrinsically unsuited to Africa. As Toyin Falola (2001) has demonstrated, some of these proposed political frameworks drew upon
currents of African intellectual thought that can be traced back to the
nineteenth century. Other aspects of these narratives were drawn from
more recent experiences. Most notably, controversial elections and civil
wars in countries such as Nigeria were cited as evidence that heated
political competition, the heartbeat of multiparty democracy, would in-
evitably generate instability. To protect against this perceived risk, leaders proposed a variety of new institutional "solutions"—in some cases
banning all political parties full stop. This was common under more
repressive forms of military rule, and also came to pass in Uganda after
1986, where the new "revolutionary" government of Uganda's National

Resistance Movement (see Chapter 4) introduced what was said to be a new type of state—the Movement System. In this political dispensation, all Ugandans were members of the Movement and could contest for power on the basis of individual merit alone. Because everyone belonged to the Movement and political parties were seen as being divisive, all parties were banned so that officially there was therefore no "ruling party." However, critics argued that this "no-party democracy" was little more than a rebranding exercise, and that in reality the Movement was a ruling party in all but name (Mugaju and Oloka-Onyango 2004).

These efforts to curtail opposition reflected a broader refusal to accept dissent and criticism. As David M. Anderson has argued, many post-independence nationalist leaders rapidly came to see themselves, and their movements, as the natural embodiment and sole legitimate rulers, of the new state. Kenya's ruling Kenya African National Union (KANU), for example, understood itself not as a political party per se but as the representative of all Kenyans and of Kenyan independence and statehood (Anderson 2005). Partly as a result, the language of unity was colored by the intimidating slogans and actions of ruling parties that depicted their supporters as loyal and their rivals as treasonous. In many cases, opposition parties—such as Kenya's Africa Democratic Union—found they had little choice but to dissolve and merge with the sole, unifying party of government to avoid being persecuted or accused of acting against the national interest (Anderson 2005). In Malawi, President for Life Hastings Kamuzu Banda pursued a similar strategy, adopting the motto "Unity, Loyalty, Obedience, and Discipline."

Fear of conflict and instability meant that while these narratives were clearly exploitative, they also resonated with many citizens, especially when they were disseminated through a wide array of networks. One-party states like that of Tanzania emerged out of anticolonial nationalist politics—a context in which intellectuals, business elites, trade unions, local chiefs, churches, mosques, women's movements, and youth groups had variously joined together in a collective effort to secure independence. Once in power, this provided nationalist regimes with access to wide networks of influential nonstate actors and organizations through which the mantra of the ruling party could be "broadcast" nationwide via pulpits, marketplaces, and local gatherings. As part of this process, discourses around unity and community were developed in dialogue with influential social groups, and so enjoyed genuine credibility. In Tanzania, for example, women's movements played a key role in the anticolonial struggle and, subsequently, in promoting the *ujamaa* philosophy (Geiger 1997).

Many citizens across post-independence Africa also felt genuine appreciation and respect for the African leaders who had overseen the securing of independence. The range of titles and honorifics accorded to authoritarian leaders around this time, as shown in Box 2.2, therefore not only served as crude propaganda but also as a genuine representation of how some communities thought about their leaders, and their right to govern. One such honorific presented the president as the unifying father of the nation. This was a particularly compelling narrative in states such as Somalia, Cameroon, and Tanzania, which came into being—in 1960, 1961, and 1964, respectively—through the merger of formerly separate colonial entities. Pre-1960 Somalia had been composed of Italian and British colonies, while the creation of Cameroon in 1961 involved the joining of a former French territory and part of Britain's British Cameroons colony. Cameroon's first president, Ahmadou Ahidjio, was literally the father of the nation (the title he often used), in the sense that he had played a major role in lobbying for some of British Cameroons to join the new Federal Republic of Cameroon. Cognizant of this critical aspect of Ahidjio's legitimacy, his successor—Paul Biya—also adopted the *Pére de la Nation* (father of the nation) moniker, which was used by Cameroonian artists in a song composed in celebration of his thirtieth year in power in 2012. These patriarchal titles have often been bolstered by the promulgation of parallel discourses around founding presidents' wives as "mothers of the nation." This is, for example, how "Mama" Ngina Kenyatta—the wife of Kenya's first president, Jomo Kenyatta, and mother of its fourth, Uhuru Kenyatta—has been known since Kenyan independence.

## Africanization

Restoring, and defending, indigenous African rule after years of colonialism represented a second—related—ideology that was promoted by authoritarian regimes to establish their legitimacy. For leaders such as Guinea's Ahmed Sékou Touré, one-party rule was justified as the most effective means to stave off persistent efforts of sabotage on the part of the jilted former colonial power. Guinea, alone among French African colonies, had opted for early independence from Paris and cut ties entirely with France in 1965. Touré presented himself to Guinean citizens as a perennial defender of their freedoms, using domestic propaganda and imagery to remind them of his descent from a famous nineteenth-century armed resister of French imperialism, Samori Ture (Schmidt 2007).

Other authoritarian rulers sought to portray themselves as chiefs to underline the "return" of political power in Africa from besuited foreigners to traditional precolonial elders. On his tours across the country, Malawi's Banda—who took on the title *Ngwazi*, meaning chief of chiefs (see Box 2.3)—always carried with him a lion-tail fly whisk, a traditional symbol of chiefly authority. The same is true of Kenya's Jomo Kenyatta, whose successor, Daniel arap Moi, was rarely seen without his *kifimbo*, a staff associated with chiefs and healers that was also used frequently by Nyerere in Tanzania.

### Box 2.3    Titles Used by African Authoritarian Leaders

The titles used by, or about, authoritarian leaders help to shed light on how they are, or wish to be, viewed both domestically and internationally. Here we present a selection of titles used by African authoritarians during the 1960s and 1970s that demonstrate the significance of ideas of unity, national independence, and chiefly authority in these leaders' efforts to legitimize their rule:

- His Excellency, President for Life, Field Marshal Al Hadji Doctor Idi Amin Dada, VC, DSO, MC, Lord of All the Beasts of the Earth and Fishes of the Seas and Conqueror of the British Empire in Africa in General and Uganda in Particular
- His Imperial Majesty Bokassa I, Emperor of Central Africa by the will of the Central African people, united within the national political party, the *Mouvemente pour l'évolution sociale de l'Afrique Noire* (MESAN)
- *Mobutu Sese Seko Ngbendu Wa Za Banga* (the warrior who knows no defeat because of his endurance and inflexible will, and is all powerful, leaving fire in his wake as he goes from conquest to conquest [Ngbendu]): President Mobutu Sese Seko of Zaire
- *Le Pére de la Nation* (father of the nation [French]): President Ahmadou Ahidjio of Cameroon
- *Responsible Suprême de la Révolution* (supreme chief of the revolution [French]): President Sékou Touré of Guinea
- *Grand Syli* (mighty elephant in French/Soso): President Ahmed Sékou Touré of Guinea
- *Mwalimu* (teacher [Swahili]) and *Baba wa Taifa* (father of the nation [Swahili]): Julius Nyerere of Tanzania

- *Osagyefo* (a chiefly Akan title meaning "redeemer"): President Kwame Nkrumah of Ghana
- *Ngwazi* (chief of chiefs or great lion [Chichewa]): President Hastings Kamuzu Banda of Malawi
- *Mzee* (elder [Swahili]): President Jomo Kenyatta of Kenya
- *Nyayo* (footsteps [Swahili]): President Daniel arap Moi of Kenya

This final honorific had a double meaning. On the one hand, it emphasized that Moi was the chosen, legitimate successor of Kenya's first president, Jomo Kenyatta, who died in 1978; Moi was "following in Kenyatta's footsteps." On the other hand, it underlined Moi's broader philosophy of African leadership, which was based around obediently following the leader and his will.

Zaïre's Joseph-Désiré Mobutu, who banned Western suits and dress in 1971, implemented perhaps the most comprehensive effort to "restore" traditional, African rule. His *retour à l'authenticité* (return to authenticity) ideology focused around rejecting Western customs and traditions and embracing the parts of Africa's "rich cultural heritage ... that adapt themselves well to modern life." *Authenticité* was a primarily symbolic and superficial exercise which nonetheless affected the everyday lives of most citizens in a number of ways. Congo's official name, for example, was changed (to Zaïre)—to better reflect the native Kikongo word for the Congo River—as were the names of many cities and the national currency. Zaïrians were encouraged to abandon Western or Christian names in favor of "African" names, with Mobutu leading by example in becoming Mobutu Sese Seko in 1972, and heavy restrictions were placed on the operation of religious groups considered to be foreign (Wrong 2000).

Lingering not so subtly behind many of these narratives on unity, chiefly authority, and self-reliance, however, was the question of who had the right to determine the country's identity and future path. Defining someone as "unKenyan" or "unZaïrian" was one way to call into question their legitimacy and justify using force against them. Opponents arguing in favor of democracy could also be harshly dismissed on the basis that they represented a threat to political stability and much needed economic development. The rhetoric of unity and consensus therefore did little to prevent the identification and persecution of minorities. In this way, governing ideologies and authoritarian politics reinforced one another: insofar as they emphasized "unifying" single-party rule and "traditional" lifetime presidencies over pluralism and a population's ability to vote out their leaders, the ideas that underpinned authoritarian rule in Africa during the 1960s and 1970s were fundamentally antidemocratic. As Mobutu once argued, *"dans notre tradition africaine, il n'y a jamais deux chefs"* ("in our African tradition, there are never two chiefs").

## FREEDOM

Critical and democratic traditions continued alongside the ideas that underpinned authoritarian rule, but they were often forced underground. Along with unity, freedom had been one of the main rallying cries of nationalist movements (Cheeseman 2015: Introduction), and many opposition leaders were quick to point out that while colonial rule had been defeated, personal freedom remained elusive. Individuals and groups that sought to challenge authoritarian rule often had to work secretly in order to survive, as direct challenges to the president could result in arrest or worse. But this did not stop a number of different intellectuals, movements, and student groups from speaking out for freedom.

One of the most important statements in defense of liberty was the the Freedom Charter of the South African Congress Alliance - which included the African National Congress (ANC) in South Africa. This was accepted as the definitive statement of the ANC's guiding principles in 1955. By this point, South Africa had been granted independence from the United Kingdom, but the country remained under the control of the white minority, which included both English speakers and Afrikaners—a group that descended from Dutch settlers who first arrived in the country in the seventeenth and eighteenth century and by the 1940s considered themselves to be South African.

The general elections of 1948—in which only whites were allowed to vote—brought the National Party (NP) to power. The NP had been established in 1914 to represent the interests of the Afrikaner community. In the 1940s this meant reinforcing white privilege and maintaining the unity of the Afrikaner group, which had come under threat as a result of growing inequality and the growing "poor white problem." The NP's solution to both goals was the policy of *apartheid*— "separateness" in English.

Apartheid, as discussed above, was a form of repression that had many similarities to the model of racial segregation operated by previous South Africa governments, but took the idea of white supremacy to a new extreme. Under apartheid, economic, political, and cultural discrimination against nonwhite communities intensified through legislation such as the 1949 Prohibition of Mixed Marriages Act, the 1950 Immorality Amendment Act, and the Pass Laws, which prohibited people of different races from having sexual relations or getting married and sought to tightly regulate the movement and activities of nonwhite communities. For example, one of the main goals of the apartheid system was to create "homelands" for black ethnic groups that were located far from the cities and the parts of the country in which the white population lived.

A number of organizations emerged to resist the policies of segregation and later apartheid, the best known of which is the ANC, which was formed in 1912 and was initially called the South African Native National Congress. The ANC aimed to give voting rights to black and mixed-race Africans, but it was initially a relatively small organization and adopted a cautious approach. It was only later, when the ANC was remodeled as a mass movement under the tutelage of the ANC Youth League (founded in 1944 and led by future South African president Nelson Mandela between 1950 and 1960) that it came to play a key role in the struggle against apartheid rule, and in South African politics more broadly.

One of the most important protests supported by the ANC during this period was the Defiance Campaign Against Unjust Laws. The Defiance Campaign, which emerged out of an ANC conference in December 1951, was led by Mandela and others, including Walter Sisulu and David Bopape, and was also supported by other nonwhite groups such as the South African Indian Congress. The aim of the campaign was to undermine apartheid rule by refusing to comply with legislation that was manifestly unjust. This might mean going to parts of the country that blacks were not allowed to live in, or refusing to carry pass books, which were a kind of internal passport that black people had to carry with them at all times when in "white" areas, and which determined where people could and could not go. All told, it is estimated that at least 8,000 people were arrested during the protests.

However, despite the sacrifices made by so many, the National Party refused to back down and instead passed a series of new laws and legislative amendments that created even greater restrictions on the lives of black people, including the establishment of a completely separate system of inferior education. It was in this context that the ANC and its allies set about drafting the Freedom Charter, which integrated the demands of ordinary people for greater freedoms with the movement's concern for economic equality and a fair distribution of national resources into one powerful statement of belief (Box 2.4).

## Box 2.4  The African National Congress and the Freedom Charter

In 1955, the ANC sent out tens of thousands of volunteers to collect the "freedom demands" of ordinary people. These were combined with the ideas and beliefs of ANC leaders into a document called the Freedom Charter, which was officially adopted as the definitive statement of the ANC's guiding principles at a Congress of the People on June 26, 1955. In addition to freedom, one of the main demands set out in the document is for economic equality, which reflects the commitment of many ANC leaders to a form of socialism—the belief that the commanding heights of the economy should be owned and regulated by the community as a whole, rather than just a small group. Although the meeting of around 3,000 delegates was disrupted by police on its second day, the Charter had already been read out by this point. Following each of the sections set out here, the crowd called out *Mayibuye! iAfrica!* to signal their approval. *Mayibuye* is a Zulu word that means "bring back what is lost," so when used in conjunction with "Africa," the slogan means "bring back the Africa which has been lost."

### The Freedom Charter

*We, the People of South Africa, declare for all our country and the world to know: that South Africa belongs to all who live in it, black and white, and that no government can justly claim authority unless it is based on the will of all the people; that our people have been robbed of their birthright to land, liberty and peace by a form of government founded on injustice and inequality; that our country will never be prosperous or free until all our people live in brotherhood, enjoying equal rights and opportunities; that only a democratic state, based on the will of all the people, can secure to all their birthright without distinction of colour, race, sex or belief; And therefore, we, the people of South Africa, black and white together— equals, countrymen and brothers—adopt this Freedom Charter. And we pledge ourselves to strive together, sparing neither strength nor courage, until the democratic changes here set out have been won.*

### The People Shall Govern!

*Every man and woman shall have the right to vote for and to stand as a candidate for all bodies which make laws; All people shall be entitled to take part in the administration of the country; The rights of the people shall be the same, regardless of race, colour or sex; All bodies of minority rule, advisory boards, councils and authorities shall be replaced by democratic organs of self-government.*

## All National Groups Shall Have Equal Rights!

*There shall be equal status in the bodies of state, in the courts and in the schools for all national groups and races; All people shall have equal right to use their own languages, and to develop their own folk culture and customs; All national groups shall be protected by law against insults to their race and national pride; The preaching and practice of national, race or colour discrimination and contempt shall be a punishable crime; All apartheid laws and practices shall be set aside.*

## The People Shall Share in the Country's Wealth!

*The national wealth of our country, the heritage of all South Africans, shall be restored to the people; The mineral wealth beneath the soil, the banks and monopoly industry shall be transferred to the ownership of the people as a whole; All other industry and trade shall be controlled to assist the well-being of the people; All people shall have equal rights to trade where they choose, to manufacture and to enter all trades, crafts and professions.*

## The Land Shall Be Shared among Those Who Work It!

*Restrictions of land ownership on a racial basis shall be ended, and all the land redivided amongst those who work it, to banish famine and land hunger; The state shall help the peasants with implements, seed, tractors and dams to save the soil and assist the tillers; Freedom of movement shall be guaranteed to all who work on the land; All shall have the right to occupy land wherever they choose; People shall not be robbed of their cattle, and forced labour and farm prisons shall be abolished.*

## All Shall Be Equal Before the Law!

*No one shall be imprisoned, deported or restricted without a fair trial; No one shall be condemned by the order of any Government official; The courts shall be representative of all the people;*

*Imprisonment shall be only for serious crimes against the people, and shall aim at re-education, not vengeance; The police force and army shall be open to all on an equal basis and shall be the helpers and protectors of the people; All laws which discriminate on grounds of race, color or belief shall be repealed.*

## All Shall Enjoy Equal Human Rights!

*The law shall guarantee to all their right to speak, to organise, to meet together, to publish, to preach, to worship and to educate their children; The privacy of the house from police raids shall be protected by law; All shall be free to travel without restriction from countryside to town, from province to province, and from South Africa abroad; Pass Laws, permits and all other laws restricting these freedoms shall be abolished.*

## There Shall Be Work and Security!

*All who work shall be free to form trade unions, to elect their officers and to make wage agreements with their employers; The state shall recognise the right and duty of all to work, and to draw full unemployment benefits; Men and women of all races shall receive equal pay for equal work; There shall be a forty-hour working week, a national minimum wage, paid annual leave, and sick leave for all workers, and maternity leave on full pay for all working mothers; Miners, domestic workers, farm workers and civil servants shall have the same rights as all others who work; Child labour, compound labour, the tot system and contract labour shall be abolished.*

## The Doors of Learning and of Culture Shall Be Opened!

*The government shall discover, develop and encourage national talent for the enhancement of our cultural life; All the cultural treasures of mankind shall be open to all, by free exchange of books, ideas and contact with other lands; The aim of education shall be to teach the youth to love their people and their culture, to honour human brotherhood, liberty and peace; Education shall be free, compulsory, universal and equal for all children; Higher education and technical training shall be opened to all by means of state allowances and scholarships awarded on the basis of merit; Adult illiteracy shall be ended by a mass state education plan; Teachers shall have all the rights of other citizens; The colour bar in cultural life, in sport and in education shall be abolished.*

### There Shall Be Houses, Security, and Comfort!

*All people shall have the right to live where they choose, to be decently housed, and to bring up their families in comfort and security; Unused housing space to be made available to the people; Rent and prices shall be lowered, food plentiful and no one shall go hungry; A preventive health scheme shall be run by the state; Free medical care and hospitalisation shall be provided for all, with special care for mothers and young children; Slums shall be demolished, and new suburbs built where all have transport, roads, lighting, playing fields, creches and social centres; The aged, the orphans, the disabled and the sick shall be cared for by the state; Rest, leisure and recreation shall be the right of all; Fenced locations and ghettoes shall be abolished, and laws which break up families shall be repealed.*

### There Shall Be Peace and Friendship!

*South Africa shall be a fully independent state, which respects the rights and sovereignty of all nations; South Africa shall strive to maintain world peace and the settlement of all international disputes by negotiation—not war; Peace and friendship amongst all our people shall be secured by upholding the equal rights, opportunities and status of all; The people of the protectorates— Basutoland, Bechuanaland and Swaziland—shall be free to decide for themselves their own future; The right of all the peoples of Africa to independence and self-government shall be recognized and shall be the basis of close co-operation.*

*Let all who love their people and their country now say, as we say here:*

*"THESE FREEDOMS WE WILL FIGHT FOR, SIDE BY SIDE, THROUGHOUT OUR LIVES, UNTIL WE HAVE WON OUR LIBERTY."*

*Adopted at the Congress of the People, Kliptown, South Africa, on June 26, 1955.*

Opposition leaders and intellectuals in other countries also lobbied for greater freedoms. In Kenya, the government became increasingly authoritarian after Vice President Daniel arap Moi replaced Jomo Kenyatta as president upon the latter's death in 1978. This was especially the case after a failed coup attempt against Moi in 1982, which left him paranoid and fearful. In response to the president's efforts to consolidate his authority by introducing a constitutional amendment that banned all opposition parties, an underground resistance movement known as the *Mwakenya* movement emerged. *Mwakenya* was short for *Muungano wa Wazalendo wa Kenya*, or the Union of Nationalists to Liberate Kenya. It was led by dissidents and academics and was particularly popular on university campuses, most notably the University of Nairobi.

*Mwakenya* organized talks and published leaflets in which they criticized the government for corruption and the abuse of power and advocated for an equal distribution of the country's wealth and resources. However, the movement was increasingly forced underground as a result of Moi's refusal to accept criticism, while influential authors and critical voices were publicly linked to the movement in an attempt to intimidate them. For example, in 1986 Ngũgĩ wa Thiong'o, the country's best-known novelist, was accused by a member of Parliament of leading the *Mwakenya* movement. Such intimidation had considerable impact because by this point it was clear that the regime's threat to strike down its opponents was not an idle one: Ngũgĩ had previously been detained between 1977 and 1978, and he understood only too well that the government had the capacity to imprison people for long periods on the basis of weak evidence and dubious charges.

During the 1980s, many of those suspected of being part of *Mwakenya* were accused of trying to overthrow the government and arrested, often without evidence. While in prison they were then treated horrendously in an attempt to force them to provide information on the movement and to confess to things that in many cases they had not done. The brutal tactics used by the regime were confirmed by Moi himself, when on a visit to London in 1989 he told a student gathering: "We only torture detained members of the disruptive dissident group, *Mwakenya*. Otherwise how are we going to get important information from them?" As a result of such repression, the movement collapsed, though its legacy lived on.

The experience of South Africa in the 1950s and 1960s, and of Kenya in the 1970s and 1980s, demonstrates that the efforts of African opposition groups and intellectuals to resist authoritarian rule were rarely successful in the short term. In South Africa, apartheid survived until 1994, when negotiations between the NP and the ANC led to a transition to majority rule and elections that brought Nelson Mandela to power. Daniel arap Moi was also able to retain power for a remarkably long period in Kenya, only standing down in 2002 after having served as president for twenty-four years. But as Toyin Falola (2001) has suggested, while the movements described here were not immediately effective, by contesting authoritarianism and arguing that a different kind of government was possible, they laid the foundations for the democratic openings of the 1990s.

The Freedom Charter, for example, played an important role in the antiapartheid struggle. The principles it set out for freedom, equality, and nonracialism shaped the approach of the ANC in future years. Moreover, when the ANC was banned and forced into exile in 1960s, many of the organizations that emerged to replace it, such as the United Democratic Front (UDF), embraced the core elements of the Freedom Charter and became known as "Charterist." Some ANC supporters have complained that the party later abandoned its commitment to economic equality as a result of a series of compromises that its leaders made in order to negotiate an end to apartheid, which effectively allowed the white community to retain the vast majority of the land and wealth accumulated under authoritarian rule. However, the fact that the guiding principles of the new ANC government were rooted in a document that privileged inclusion and freedom – and that influential members of the movement continued to believe in these ideals – was one reason that South Africa subsequently emerged out of a divisive and authoritarian past to become one of the most liberal and democratic states on the continent.

## CONCLUSION: PERFORMING POWER

The irony of the Africanization ideologies put forward by many authoritarian rulers was that these leaders were often far removed from the societies they sought to govern. Malawi's Banda was as famous for his Savile Row suits, Homburg hats, and the Eton-inspired Kamuzu Academy[1] he founded as he was for his lion-tail fly whisk. Even "Zaïre," the "local" name for Congo selected by Mobutu, was actually derived from a Portuguese corruption of an indigenous word. Mobutu also prided himself on his vast collections of imported pink champagne, caviar, and Louis XIV furniture. The immense palace he had had constructed in northern Zaïre was referred to by critics as the "Versailles of the jungle."

Moreover, most African leaders of the 1960s and 1970s spent significant parts of their twenties and thirties outside the continent. Kwame Nkrumah lived in the United States and United Kingdom between the

---

[1] Founded in 1981 and still in operation, Kamuzu Academy was "modelled on the best in the English independent boarding school tradition" and still includes Latin or Greek as a compulsory subject for all students (http://kamuzuacademy.com/history.html; accessed September 6, 2019).

ages of twenty-six and thirty-eight, returning to Ghana (at that time still known as the Gold Coast) only two years before forming the nationalist political party, the Convention People's Party. Léopold Senghor—who ruled Senegal for twenty years—spoke of his "sixteen years of wandering" as a professor, soldier, and Senegalese **deputy** in France between the ages of twenty-two and thirty-eight. Jomo Kenyatta traveled to Britain in 1929 at the age of thirty-two, studying at University College London and the London School of Economics and returning to Kenya permanently nearly eighteen years later. Hastings Banda received his tertiary education in the United States and United Kingdom and practiced as a doctor in Newcastle, London, and Scotland between 1941 and 1945.

This does not mean that these men were necessarily "out of touch" with the communities they later came to rule; they maintained regular contact with domestic political organizations and networks and represented them at international pan-African and anticolonial fora. Nor is it a surprise that intelligent, ambitious future leaders looked beyond Africa to secure further education and training in the dying years of European imperialism. Colonial governments had invested very little in African universities, and access to those that did exist was often politicized or heavily restricted.

What it does mean, though, is that most African rulers during this period were deeply conscious of how different *audiences* perceived them. During their formative years, these individuals negotiated the construction of personal and political networks in Africa, Europe, and North America. They also worked hard to establish credibility and authority with everyone from elites and diplomats to workers and peasants. This made them aware of the salience—or weakness—of particular ideas, norms, and identities in different contexts, and the importance of adapting to these contexts for their own political survival. As the next two chapters demonstrate, many authoritarian leaders relied heavily on external relationships to sustain their rule, and the ways in which they portrayed themselves in these interactions often differed markedly from how they did so at home.

## REFERENCES

Anderson, David M. "'Yours in Struggle for *Majimbo*': Nationalism and the Party Politics of Decolonization in Kenya, 1955–64." *Journal of Contemporary History* 40, no. 3 (July 2005): 547–64.

Cheeseman, Nic. *Democracy in Africa: Successes, Failures, and the Struggle for Political Reform.* Cambridge: Cambridge University Press, 2015.

Cheeseman, Nic, and Brian Klaas. *How to Rig an Election*. New Haven, CT: Yale University Press, 2018.

Clapham, Christopher. *Transformation and Continuity in Revolutionary Ethiopia*. Cambridge: Cambridge University Press, 1988.

Decker, Alice C. *In Idi Amin's Shadow: Women, Gender and Militarism in Uganda*. Harrogate, UK: Combined Academic Publishers, 2014.

Falola, Toyin. *Nationalism and African Intellectuals*. Rochester, NY: University of Rochester Press, 2001.

Geiger, Susan. *TANU Women: Gender and Culture in the Making of Tanganyikan Nationalism*. Portsmouth, NH: Heinemann, 1997.

Herbst, Jeffrey. *States and Power in Africa: Comparative Lessons in Authority and Control*. Princeton, NJ: Princeton University Press, 2014.

Molony, Thomas. *Nyerere: The Early Years*. Suffolk, UK: James Currey, 2014.

Mugaju, Justus, and Joe Oloka-Onyango, eds. *No-Party Democracy in Uganda: Myths and Realities*. Kampala: Fountain Publishers, 2004.

Schmidt, Elizabeth. *Cold War and Decolonization in Guinea, 1946–1958*. Athens: Ohio University Press, 2007.

Woldegiorgis, Dawit. *Red Tears: War, Famine and Revolution in Ethiopia*. Trenton, NJ: Red Sea Press, 1989.

Wrong, Michela. *In the Footsteps of Mr Kurtz: Living on the Brink of Disaster in the Congo*. London: Zed Books, 2000.

## SUGGESTED READINGS

Crabb, John H. "The Coronation of Emperor Bokassa." *Africa Today* 25, no. 3 (July–September 1978): 25–44.

Leonardi, Cherry. *Dealing with Government in South Sudan: Histories of Chiefship, Community and State*. Oxford: James Currey, 2015.

Logan, Carolyn. "The Roots of Resilience: Exploring Popular Support for African Traditional Authorities." *African Affairs* 112, no. 448 (July 2013): 353–76.

Kapuscinski, Ryszard. *The Emperor: Downfall of an Autocrat*. London: Penguin, 2006.

Kenyatta, Jomo. *Facing Mount Kenya*. London: Harvill Secker, 1938.

Mbembe, Achille. *On the Postcolony*. Oakland: University of California Press, 2001.

Van Beurden, Sarah. "The Art of (Re) Possession: Heritage and the Cultural Politics of Congo's Decolonization." *The Journal of African History* 56, no. 1 (March 2015): 143–64.

# It's the Economy, Stupid!

*The Economic Foundations of Authoritarian
Rule, 1970–88*

Isabel dos Santos of Angola has often been said to be one of the most impressive young business leaders on the African continent. With a personal fortune of some $2.6 billion, she is Africa's wealthiest woman and has a track record in developing businesses in a number of areas, most notably telecommunications. So in some ways it was no surprise when the Undergraduate Association for African Peace and Development of Yale University (YAAPD) invited her to speak at its annual conference in 2018. In her talk, dos Santos put her success down to hard work.

However, critics on social media were quick to point out a different story. As the oldest daughter of Angola's longtime former president, José Eduardo dos Santos (in power 1979–2017), much of dos Santos's wealth was directly transferred to her by her father, who gifted her stakes in several companies. And while it is true that some of her income was generated when she was the head of the state oil firm Sonangol, this too was a position that she was given by her illustrious parent.

Isabel dos Santos is not, of course, the only daughter of a wealthy politician to put her success—somewhat disingenuously—down to hard work rather than the patronage of a billionaire parent. In her 2017 book, *Women Who Work* Ivanka Trump, US President Donald Trump's eldest daughter, explained her professional accomplishments—she is, at the time of writing, worth over $300 million—as the consequence of being "passionate" and "work [ing] hard." Donald Trump himself once told a New Hampshire audience that building his property empire had "not been easy," noting that he started off with only "a small loan of a million dollars" from his father. The difference between the Trumps and dos Santoses – until Trump came to power in America at least – is that the latter derived their wealth from directly managing, and apportioning off, the assets of the state itself. The same process has also enriched the sons of presidents and government ministers in many authoritarian African states.

Isabel dos Santos is not alone in personally benefitting from Angola's oil wealth. Through a complex range of patronage networks, the country's ruling party, the People's Movement for the Liberation of Angola (MPLA), constructed an elaborate system of clientelism—the exchange of economic resources and opportunities in return for political support—in which a broad range of elites were co-opted into the political system.

By distributing oil rents to secure the support of key families and constituencies, and allowing some resources to flow down to the party's supporters, the ruling party set about consolidating its hold on power following the end of a protracted civil war that lasted until 2002. As Ricardo Soares de Oliveira (2015) has argued, it is the country's vast oil reserves—9.5 billion barrels of proven holdings—that has empowered the MPLA to pursue a form of **illiberal state-building** that has largely ignored civil liberties and political rights.

With so much income generated by the sale of oil, the Angolan government has been empowered to turn a deaf ear to criticism from abroad and closer to home—at least until the price of oil crashed by about 60 percent between June 2014 and January 2015. Thereafter, managing Angola's petro-state became significantly more difficult, because the level of expenditure that was previously possible was no longer sustainable. As a result, the number of people who can be successfully co-opted into the system has fallen, causing fresh problems for the regime.

The Angolan example is illustrative of a broader trend. One of the most famous patterns in political science is that wealthier countries tend to be more politically stable. Research conducted in the 1990s by Jose Antonio Cheibub and his colleagues (1996) revealed that authoritarian states with economies that produce more than US$20,000 dollars' worth of goods and services per citizen a year almost always survive.[1]

---

[1] These figures have been adjusted for inflation—they were $6,000 and $1,000 at the time Cheibub et al. were writing.

By contrast, authoritarian regimes that emerge in countries with a GDP per capita of less than $3,000 almost always collapse. This correlation suggests a very straightforward relationship between national wealth and productivity and the durability of a government: a bigger economy means better political prospects.

In the 1970s and 1980s, the economic conditions that governments faced did indeed influence their prospects for survival. There are two main ways in which this happened. The first is that governments need resources to be able to fund their activities, whether this is providing services to their citizens, rewarding supporters, or simply paying the wages of the police and army. Such resources are particularly significant for authoritarian regimes, because they find it more difficult to generate democratic legitimacy though elections. It is therefore important for them to be able to sustain public support by delivering goods to key individuals and constituencies, and to be able to repress opposition when it emerges. As the Angolan case demonstrates, sustaining the costs of authoritarian rule is far easier when government income is consistently high.

The second way that economic factors shape political developments is related to the process through which the government accesses its income. If key resources are difficult to produce and require the involvement of thousands of workers and the cooperation of trade unions, governments may have to negotiate—for example, over wages and working conditions—in order to secure the funds they require. Similarly, if a government depends on aid from Western states to survive, it may need to adopt certain policies favored by those states, such as "good governance" reforms. By contrast, governments that control valuable natural resources such as oil and gas do not need to negotiate with international partners or domestic groups in the same way, which is why they so often feature authoritarian governments.

It is therefore significant that the sources of government revenue in Africa during the 1970s and 1980s were very different from those in many other parts of the world. In Europe, North America, Latin America, and East Asia, governments secured the majority of their income through direct taxes and sales taxes in the 1970s. In other words, their revenue flows depended on the tax that citizens paid on their wages, and the tax that they paid on goods and services. In those states that held reasonable quality elections, this meant that the governments had to take into account what citizens were and were not willing to pay for and to moderate their policies accordingly.

By contrast, African states during the same period generated most of their revenue through trade taxes. In other words, their income came from taxing goods as they were exported out of the country and as they were imported in to it. This led to the rise of what Fred Cooper (2002), Julia Gallagher (2018), and others have called "gate-keeper states"—governments that are dependent for their survival not on the support of their own people, but on their control of the "gate" between their country and the wider world. In the 1970s, being able to control the border was important because the sale of goods such as tea and coffee generated considerable income. When much of the continent began to experience economic difficulties in the 1980s, control of the "gate" remained important, because it was by engaging with international partners that governments could access the foreign aid and loans that they needed to survive.

The significance of the economy to the potential for democratic and authoritarian politics has echoes of the famous phrase often said of the key driver of election outcomes in the United States—"It's the economy, stupid."[2] But it is important to keep in mind that while a state's economy shapes its political development, it does not determine exactly how history will unfold.

## OIL AND THE POLITICS OF SURVIVAL

The relationship between the economy and the political prospects for a country can be seen most starkly when it comes to the impact of oil. From the mid-1970s to the mid-2000s, there were nine main oil-producing countries in Africa: Angola, Cameroon, Chad, Cote d'Ivoire, Equatorial Guinea, Gabon, Nigeria, Republic of Congo, and Sudan (see Table 3.1). Throughout this period, the vast majority of these states were ranked as "not free" by Freedom House, an American think tank that evaluates respect for civil liberties and political rights in every country in the world on an annual basis. At the same time, the two countries that escaped this rating in 1975 and 1995, and the three in 2005, were only evaluated as being "Partly Free." This means not a single one of these states was rated as "free"—even after the reintroduction of multiparty politics in the early 1990s.

---

[2] The term is believed to have been coined by James Carville, a campaign strategist of Bill Clinton in 1992, and was intended to focus the minds of the campaign team on key issues.

**TABLE 3.1**   Major Oil Producers and Political Freedom, 1975–2005[3]

|  | 1975 | | 1995 | | 2005 | |
|---|---|---|---|---|---|---|
|  | % of GDP | FH* | % of GDP | FH | % of GDP | FH |
| Nigeria | 24 | Not free | 34 | Not free | 38 | Partly free |
| Angola | 26* | Not free | 52 | Not free | 65 | Not free |
| Gabon | 38 | Not free | 38 | Partly free | 54 | Partly free |
| Eq. Guinea | 0 | Not free | 22 | Not free | 79 | Not free |
| Chad | 0 | Not free | 0 | Not free | 60 | Not free |
| Congo, R. of | 18 | Partly free | 45 | Partly free | 70 | Partly free |
| Sudan | 0 | Not free | 0 | Not free | 19 | Not free |
| Cote d'Ivoire | 0 | Not free | 1 | Not free | 4 | Not free |
| Cameroon | 0 | Partly free | 6 | Not free | 8 | Not free |

*FH = Freedom House score.
**First recorded amount from 1985.

*Source*: Cheeseman (2015).

The politics of oil are well illustrated by the example of Nigeria. Oil was first discovered in Nigeria in large quantities in 1956 by the Shell-British Petroleum Development Company of Nigeria Ltd. (originally known as Shell D'Arcy), a British-Dutch company. Production began in 1958, although at this stage the flow of "black gold" was low, just 5,000 barrels per day. In 1966, Elf, a French oil company, began operating in another part of the country, producing 12,000 barrels a day. From that point onward, production began to rapidly escalate and by the mid-1980s, the country was generating over a million barrels a day, a figure that would rise further to a record of 2.5 million in 2004.

The total value of the oil exported by Nigeria over this period was remarkable. In 2017, the National Bureau of Statistics estimated that between 1961 and 2014, 32.70 billion barrels of crude oil had been produced with a total value of 118.49 trillion Naira, which is about US$0.33 trillion. As you might expect, throughout this period oil dominated the economy, regularly making up more 90 percent of the country's total revenue from all of the goods that it exported.

---

[3] Major oil finds in Ghana and Uganda occurred after this date.

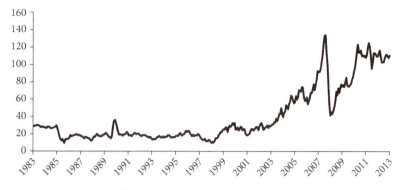

**FIGURE 3.1**   The Value of Crude Oil, 1983–2013 (price per barrel in current US$)

*Source*: Cheeseman (2015).

In addition to generating vast amounts of money for the Nigerian government, the existence of so much oil meant that the country gained in geo-strategic importance. Because oil is such a sought-after commodity, and the production of oil in the 1970s and 1980s was controlled by a relatively small number of countries, these states gained a disproportionate influence over world affairs. This was especially true when they coordinated their activities. In 1960, five of the main oil-producing states—Iran, Iraq, Kuwait, Saudi Arabia, and Venezuela—joined forces to form the Organization of the Petroleum Exporting Countries (OPEC). By deliberately restricting the supply of oil, these states were able to make it more valuable and so increase its price, bringing them even greater benefits.

Nigeria joined OPEC in 1971 in recognition of its growing importance as an oil producer and benefitted from the spike in oil prices that occurred in 1973 when the Arab producers placed an embargo on oil in a bid to punish Western countries for their support of Israel during the Yom Kippur war with Egypt. As a result of the boycott, the price of crude oil rose from $3 per barrel in 1973 to $12 per barrel in 1974. Nigeria also benefitted later that decade, in 1979, when the Iranian Revolution led to a disruption of the oil supply from that country and panic drove the price of oil to $39.50 per barrel.

The collective impact of Nigeria's oil wealth and vast size—it is the thirty-second largest country in the world by land mass and the seventh largest by population—supported the emergence of a powerful state, at least in regional terms. While the government often failed to deliver to its own citizens, as we shall see, it developed significant military capacity, and its armed forces are typically ranked as one of the top three most powerful on the continent. As a result, Nigeria is often said to be a regional hegemon in West Africa, meaning that it is able to exert a powerful influence over relations with neighboring states and developments in the area.

This has had three significant implications where authoritarian rule is concerned. First, the government has had considerable revenue at its disposal to co-opt influential individuals and so strengthen its hold on power. This is not to say that military governments in Nigeria have actually performed well in terms of providing goods and services. In many cases, waste and corruption undermined the provision of key services such as healthcare and education, and a tendency to make poor investment decisions in the boom years meant that the country's governments often struggled to sustain previous levels of expenditure, greatly frustrating the population.

But what the government was able to do with the proceeds of oil exports was to establish a complex set of patron–client relations through which regionally powerful individuals leant their support to the government in return for being allowed to become incredible wealthy. Richard Joseph (1987) had described this as a system of "prebendalism," in which political leaders felt that they had a right to take a share of government revenues and use them to benefit themselves, their families, and people from the same religious and ethnic group. Through this system, which has also been referred to as a neo-patrimonial model (see Chapter 2), a set of powerful fixers with the capacity to control political developments in their part of the country emerged. In turn, the personal networks controlled by these figures, known locally as "godfathers," have helped to sustain successive governments in power—so long as there is sufficient revenue to keep the wheels well-greased.

Second, the ability of the government to fund the repressive machinery of the state—most notably the army and security forces—enabled a succession of military leaders to establish a powerful stranglehold over the political landscape from the 1960s until the end of the 1990s. Third, the country's geo-strategic importance has often muted criticism of its regimes' democratic deficiencies and spending excesses from the international community (see Box 3.1). This has not always been the case, but even when Western governments have spoken out against human rights abuses, the presence of oil has empowered the Nigerian government to form new alliances with other international players.

## Box 3.1   Theft, Excess, and Impunity in Africa's Gatekeeper States

Being able to rely primarily on external resources rather than internal legitimation has meant that many authoritarian gatekeeper regimes in Africa have felt that they can loot state resources and spend national budgets at will. Nigeria's Sani Abacha became notorious for—allegedly—siphoning off billions of dollars from the Nigerian treasury to bank accounts in Europe. In recent years, Nigerian leaders have pledged to redistribute this "Abacha loot"—some of which was returned by order of the Swiss government—directly to Nigerian households. Likewise, the eldest son of oil-rich Equatorial Guinea's Teodoro Obiang Nguema Mbasogo became well-known in Paris during the 2000s for his lavish "playboy" lifestyle, expensive cars and a €107 million mansion near the Champs-Élysées, a lifestyle he could apparently afford despite his declared monthly salary of €3,200.

Perhaps the most infamous regime in this regard, however, was that of Mobutu Sese Seko in Zaïre. Mobutu—who embezzled billions of dollars during his three-decade-long presidency—spent over $100 million of Zaïre's national budget on constructing a huge palace in Gbadolite, northern Zaïre, complete with a swimming pool and an international airport large enough to land Concorde airplanes. When being entertained, Mobutu's guests could enjoy Tattinger champagne and salmon imported from Europe circulated on conveyor belts, while on Mobutu's fifty-fifth birthday, in 1985, one of France's most celebrated pastry chefs was flown to Zaïre on Concorde with a birthday cake for the president. Perhaps unsurprisingly, in one of his obituaries, Mobutu was described as "Africa's greatest kleptocrat."

Such conspicuous consumption also served another purpose for authoritarian rulers because it demonstrated to current—and future—political "clients" that loyalty to the "big man" would pay far better than being in the opposition ever could. Public displays of wealth also bolstered the kind of governing narratives of supreme chieftancy explored in Chapter 2; the "warrior who is all powerful"—as Mobutu referred to himself—should surely *look like* he was all powerful in his lifestyle and his absolute command of national resources. These actions nonetheless did untold damage not only to state finances and the construction of state infrastructures but also to Africa's international reputation. Even today, the continent's most diligent reformers must contend with Western media stereotypes of African leaders as corrupt kleptomaniacs.

For example, in 1995 the highly authoritarian government of Sani Abacha arrested and executed the environmental activist Ken Saro-Wiwa following a flawed trial. In response, a number of governments, including the United Kingdom and the United States, cut ties with Nigeria. This caused significant difficulties for the Abacha regime and led to growing support for an end to military rule. However, the country's oil wealth enabled Abacha to develop strong ties to China—a country that was becoming increasingly thirsty for resources, and which placed even less of an emphasis on human rights and democracy than the United Kingdom or United States. As new trading ties with Beijing replaced old ones with Washington, the government was able to secure the revenue that it needed to survive. Thus, the Nigerian government was not forced to reintroduce multiparty politics by either popular pressure or foreign intervention. Instead, it took Abacha's unexpected death in office in June 1998—what some Nigerians referred to as "the coup from heaven"—to open up a window of opportunity for those seeking political reform to push for a more democratic political system.

## TRADE UNIONS AND POLITICAL BARGAINING IN ZAMBIA

The impact of oil in Nigeria is perhaps easiest to see if we draw a comparison to the experience of other African states during this period. While oil-exporting states such as Nigeria were able to take advantage of high prices in the 1970s and 1980s, the opposite was true for oil-importing countries who suffered as the cost of fuel increased dramatically. This had a profound effect on countries such as Malawi and Tanzania, which struggled to fund fuel imports by selling less valuable crops like tea and coffee. In the late 1970s and early 1980s, this situation led many African countries to develop unsustainable trade deficits.

Zambia was one of these countries. Having gained independence under the leadership of Kenneth Kaunda and the United National Independence Party (UNIP), the country maintained a **multiparty political system** until 1972. However, in that year mounting instability within the ruling party, combined with growing public frustration and greater tensions with white minority governments such as South Africa, led Kaunda to establish a one-party state. The prohibition of opposition parties temporarily resolved the government's political problems, leaving Kaunda with three major economic challenges.

First, the country was landlocked, which increased the cost of importing and exporting goods, pushing the price of oil even higher and making Zambian products less competitive on world markets. Second, international sanctions against the white minority regime of Ian Smith in what was then called Rhodesia (now Zimbabwe) in the late 1960s and early 1970s had a negative impact on Zambia because they effectively closed down one of the most efficient routes for getting things into and out of the country.

Third, Zambia's main export, copper, was significantly less valuable than oil and, instead of rising, its price fluctuated greatly on world markets. For example, copper and cobalt had generated 54 percent of government income in 1974 but provided little between 1977 and 1979, while the cost of the country's oil imports rose from K 17.7 million in 1973 to K 122.9 million in 1980. Because Zambia depended on copper for the vast majority of its export earnings, this seriously undermined the ability of the government to maintain public services and co-opt influential sections of society. Partly as a result, the country suffered negative economic growth across its first three decades of independence—meaning that it was poorer in 1990 than it had been in 1960. Over time, this made it increasingly difficult for the Zambian government to retain political control.

The nature of the copper industry also created other kinds of constraints in terms of the need to enter into negotiations with the workers who worked on the copper mines. In Nigeria, the production of oil was largely carried out by multinational oil companies such as Shell BP, who used technology that only required a relatively small number of international experts and a slightly larger group of Nigerian workers to function. Consequently, the total number of workers did not reach much more than 1,000 people—just 0.002 percent of the total population and less than 0.01 percent of the country's workforce.[4] At the same time, the fact that much of the oil is located off the Nigerian coast meant that these workers did not live in the kind of densely populated urban areas that can give rise to a culture of more radical politics. Taken together, these factors ensured that those working in the oil sector were relatively small and easy to manage – at least, until the rise of violent localized insurgencies in the 1990s led by leaders who were angered that the communities living on or near the oil were benefiting so little from its export.

The situation in Zambia was very different. Copper mining is a labor-intensive process that requires thousands of people to work in

---

[4] The Nigerian population is estimated at 56 million in the 1970s—it is far higher today.

very cramped conditions. The rise of the copper industry in Zambia therefore triggered processes of urbanization, as people came to reside and later live near mining compounds. Miles Larmer (2006) has shown that as urban areas grew in size, workers became increasingly conscious that they shared a class identity. In other words, mineworkers came to feel a sense of solidarity with one another and to believe that their low pay and poor working conditions meant that they were being exploited by their employers. In response, they formed trade unions to represent their interests.

This was significant for two main reasons. On the one hand, the explicit rejection of "traditional" forms of leadership meant that the government could not pacify mineworkers by co-opting their chiefs, or through a system of prebendalism, as in Nigeria. As early as 1953, the vast majority of the African Mineworkers' Union voted to abolish a system of "tribal" representation based on traditional forms of authority and instead elected its own leadership. Because union leaders were selected by rank-and-file members and were often heavily criticized if they were seen to be too close to mining bosses, the government was forced to bargain with the workforce rather than simply co-opting them.

On the other hand, the sheer number of mineworkers, and their influence within urban areas, ensured that they were able to exert considerable political influence. By the early 1950s, there were already 270,000 African workers on the mines, and production could not continue if they went on strike. The mineworkers' effective organization and strategic importance within the country's most significant industry enabled them to extract a number of concessions from the government over the subsequent thirty years. These included pay increases and better working conditions—though rarely to the full satisfaction of the rank and file—and maintaining their independence from UNIP control. Along with the limited revenues collected by the government—which meant that it would have been extremely difficult to develop a powerful military on the Nigerian model even if Kaunda had wanted to—these factors ensured that for many years Zambia's one-party state rested as much on a process of negotiation than it did on ouright repression.

At the same time, the country's more fragile economic base meant that it quickly became dependent on external sources of financial assistance. Indeed, Zambia was first forced to go to the International Monetary Fund for help in 1973, and entered into a series of **structural adjustment programs** with the World Bank from 1978 onward. However, few of these programs worked, and so the country became increasingly indebted throughout the 1980s. Zambia was not alone in having this experience: as Figure 3.2 demonstrates, having enjoyed

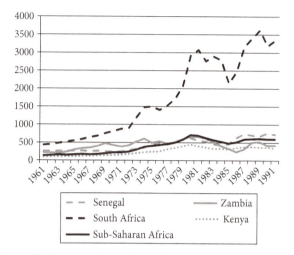

**FIGURE 3.2**    GDP per capita in selected countries (1961–91), current US$.
*Source*: World Bank.[5]

steady if unspectacular economic growth during the early 1970s, most oil-importing states suffered negative or low economic growth between the 1979 oil price shock and the early 1990s.

Despite the failure of the economic measures promoted by the International Monetary Fund and the World Bank, UNIP still had to follow some of the policies advised by these bodies because the government was constantly in need of fresh loans. This meant enforcing unpopular policies that were designed to reduce government expenditure and increase fiscal discipline—and so return the country to a more sustainable footing—such as employing fewer people in state institutions and removing expensive subsidies. The difficulty that these changes generated for UNIP is well illustrated by events in 1986, when the removal of a food subsidy led to the price of the country's staple food doubling overnight. In response, many urban residents rioted, leading to serious clashes between protestors and the security forces that resulted in a number of deaths.

UNIP never recovered and, as we shall see in the next chapter, just a few years later the one-party state was replaced by a multiparty system. Although these developments were shaped by a broad range of different domestic and international factors, they were rooted in the economic difficulties that both exacerbated opposition to the one-party state in the late 1980s and undermined Kaunda's ability to respond.

---

[5] For this and more economic data, go to https://data.worldbank.org.

## CONCLUSION: THE IMPACT OF NATURAL RESOURCES

This chapter has demonstrated that the nature of the economy plays an important role in shaping the way that leaders have to engage with their people and the potential for sustaining authoritarian forms of government. Nigeria and Zambia demonstrate just two of the different trajectories followed by African states, and others – such as predominantly agricultural economies – had their own distinctive features. But it is important to be clear that this does not mean that the economy *determines* how a country will evolve. With good management, leaders can ride out difficult economic and political conditions. Similarly, bad economic management can create serious problems for governments, even in countries blessed with valuable resources.

It is also important to note that while the presence of oil predisposed Nigeria toward a form of more repressive authoritarianism, it did not make the country politically stable. Instead, Nigeria experienced a series of coups and countercoups throughout the period from independence until the reintroduction of multiparty politics in 1999. As the oil price rose and corruption spiraled, it became clear to the country's entrepreneurs that the way to do well economically was to do well politically. By gaining control of the state—and often only by gaining control of the state—a leader and his allies could become wealthy beyond their wildest dreams. This is one reason why "gatekeeper" states have often proved to be highly unstable: the concentration of wealth and opportunities on the president and those close to him encouraged people with political and economic ambitions to do whatever it took to take power.

This was one reason that states with valuable natural resources were more likely to experience armed uprisings and civil conflict during this period, but it was not the only one. It was also true that the more repressive nature of governments in resource-rich states meant that their citizens had fewer reasons to believe that the situation could be improved through protest or negotiation. The extreme levels of economic inequality that typically went hand in hand with oil and diamonds also played a role in destabilizing these countries. In many cases, the revenue that these resources generated was largely wasted, which meant that life in a "petro-state" was often unpredictable and frustrating (see Box 3.2).

At the same time, the presence of valuable resources also helped to prolong conflict in some states. In countries in which resources could be captured—for example, when they were accessible and could

## Box 3.2    Life in a Petro-State

*This is an excerpt from a song by Sonny Okuson called "Which Way Nigeria," which was released in 1983. Okuson was a famous pop singer who became known for his protest songs. More than thirty years after it was released, "Which Way Nigeria" continues to resonate for many Nigerians.*

I want to know
which way Nigeria is heading to
many years after independence
we still find it hard to start
how long shall we be patient still we reach the promise land
let's save Nigeria
so Nigeria won't die . . .

We start to blame the government
we know everything that goes wrong
we are part of the government
let's save Nigeria
so Nigeria won't die . . .

Inefficiency and indiscipline
is ruining the country now
corruption here there and everywhere
inflation is very high
let's save Nigeria
so Nigeria won't die . . .

We make mistakes in the oil boom
not knowing that was our doom
some people now have everything
while some have nothing
let's save Nigeria so Nigeria won't fall
which way Nigeria
which way to go . . .

Our ambition to become millionaires is ruining the country down
we all want to be millionaires we want to leave in the earth
let's save Nigeria
so Nigeria won't die . . .

                                                    AMEN

easily be exploited—the leaders of armed rebel groups knew that by gaining control of resource-rich parts of the country they could raise the funds they needed to prosecute their rebellion. In turn, the greater feasibility of waging conflict helped to sustain civil wars in countries such as the Democratic Republic of Congo.

Taken together, the combination of these interrelated processes meant that while the presence of valuable natural resources may have led to more authoritarian governments, it also exposed them to greater risk of armed rebellion. In this way, resource wealth contributed to the kind of fragile authoritarianism described in previous chapters.

## REFERENCES

Cheibub, Jose Antonio, Adam Przeworski, Fernando Papaterra Limongi Neto, and Michael M. Alvarez. "What Makes Democracies Endure?" *Journal of Democracy* 7, no. 1 (1996): 39–55.

Cooper, Fred. *Africa Since 1940: The Past of the Present.* Cambridge: Cambridge University Press, 2002.

Gallagher, Julia. "Zimbabwe's Consolidation as a Gatekeeper State." *Third World Thematics: A TWQ Journal*, 3, no. 3 (2018): 439–454.

Joseph, Richard A. *Democracy and Prebendal Politics in Nigeria: The Rise and Fall of the Second Republic.* Cambridge: Cambridge University Press, 1987.

Larmer, Miles. "'The Hour Has Come at the Pit': The Mineworkers' Union of Zambia and the Movement for Multi-Party Democracy, 1982–1991." *Journal of Southern African Studies* 32, no. 1 (2006): 293–312.

Soares De Oliveira, Ricardo. *Magnificent and Beggar Land: Angola Since the Civil War.* Oxford: Oxford University Press, 2015.

Trump, Ivanka. *Women Who Work.* New York: Penguin Random House, 2017.

## SUGGESTED READINGS

Brautigam, Deborah, Odd-Helge Fjeldstad, and Mick Moore, eds. *Taxation and State-Building in Developing Countries: Capacity and Consent.* Cambridge: Cambridge University Press, 2008.

Gibbon, Peter, Yusuf Bangura, and Arve Ofstad, eds. *Authoritarianism, Democracy, and Adjustment: The Politics of Economic Reform in Africa.* Uppsala: Nordic Africa Institute, 1992.

Hamalengwa, Munyonzwe. *Class Struggles in Zambia, 1889–1989 and the Fall of Kenneth Kaunda, 1990–1991.* Lanham, MD: University Press of America, 1992.

Ihonvbere, Julius Omozuanvbo. *Economic Crisis, Civil Society, and Democratization: The Case of Zambia*. Trenton, NJ: Africa World Press, 1996.

Lewis, Peter M. "Economic Reform and Political Transition in Africa: The Quest for a Politics of Development." *World Politics* 49, no. 1 (1996): 92–129.

Obi, Cyril I. "Oil Extraction, Dispossession, Resistance, and Conflict in Nigeria's Oil-Rich Niger Delta." *Canadian Journal of Development Studies* 30, nos. 1–2 (2010): 219–36.

Van de Walle, Nicolas. *African Economies and the Politics of Permanent Crisis, 1979–1999*. Cambridge: Cambridge University Press, 2001.

White, Gordon. "Civil Society, Democratization and Development (II): Two Country Cases." *Democratization* 2, no. 2 (1995): 56–84.

Whitfield, Lindsay, Ole Therkildsen, Lars Buur, and Anne Mette Kjaer. *The Politics of African Industrial Policy: A Comparative Perspective*. New York: Cambridge University Press, 2015.

# The Tail Wagging the Dog?

*The International Community and African Authoritarianism, 1975–2000*

During the Cold War, the United States and Soviet Union competed for allies in Africa. The two superpowers offered development aid and military assistance to regimes prepared to align with one of them in their global battle against the other. Whether these regimes were democratic or authoritarian made little difference to Washington and Moscow; what mattered was a regime's loyalty and, to a lesser extent, commitment to communism (Soviet Union) or capitalism (United States). For authoritarian rulers who could not rely on rents from vast natural resources to keep them in power, therefore, playing the superpowers off against one another came to represent an appealing alternative.

Nowhere on the continent was this strategy deployed more successfully than in the Horn of Africa. In Somalia, the regime of Siad Barre enthusiastically supported the Soviet Union since Barre—who called himself *Jaale Siyaad*, or "Comrade Siad"—had come to power in a communist-inspired military coup in October 1969. As head of the new "Supreme Revolutionary Council," Barre set about establishing a ruthless, one-party dictatorship based on a combination of scientific socialism and Somali nationalism. Propped up by Moscow, his communist regime ruled through cult of personality and a fearsome elite military brigade known as the "red berets," harking back to the red star and red flag symbols of socialism since the 1917 Russian Revolution. With Soviet support, Barre was able to build one of the largest and most formidable armies in Africa and present a major threat to neighboring Ethiopia, whose eastern Ogaden region Somalia claimed.

By the spring of 1977, however, the relationship between Mogadishu and Moscow was cooling. The socialist revolution in Ethiopia eighteen months earlier (see Chapter 2) had led to the emergence of a new, communist power in the region—and the Soviet Union jumped at the opportunity to make an ally out of a country which had, under emperor Haile Selassie, been such a staunch US partner. Barre and his advisers viewed Soviet support for Ethiopia as a major betrayal and begun to put out feelers—via Somalia's ambassador in Washington—to the United States.

Over the next few months, a remarkable *volte face* was performed—the evolution of which can be traced in the extracts from leaked US embassy cables quoted in Box 4.1. Despite initial ambivalence on both sides – a high-powered Somali delegation traveled to Moscow in May to join in the sixtieth anniversary celebrations of the Russian Revolution – the United States offered, and Somalia accepted, economic aid in May. On July 12, Somalia's US ambassador presented the State Department with a "shopping list" of weapons the country would require in order to strengthen the relationship with Washington. On July 13, Somalia invaded Ethiopia, intent on annexing Ogaden. Two days later, US President Jimmy Carter "agreed in principle" to the arms request. By November, the last Soviet military advisers were expelled from Somalia, with some rerouted to Addis Ababa to assist with Ethiopia's war effort. As recently as September 1974, Somalia had been Moscow's main regional client, and Ethiopia Washington's. Now, less than three years later, the superpowers had swapped roles, providing arms, aid, and military training to their former enemies to help them defeat their former allies. Ideology, it turned out, was less important than the cold hard reality of state survival.

The ability of some authoritarian African states to extract vital economic aid and weaponry from international actors in this context has been characterized by some scholars, somewhat unflatteringly, as "the tail wagging the dog"—that is, when the less important part of something is able to control the whole thing. Despite being dependent on aid, many authoritarian African states were able to skillfully leverage their value as Cold War allies to secure critical international support during the 1970s and 1980s—and many have continued to do so since in relation to other global agendas such as the Global War on Terror.

## Box 4.1   Somalia's Cold War International Relations

*During 1977, socialist Somalia transformed itself from a Soviet ally into a US partner, leveraging the global Cold War context to jettison one superpower patron in favor of another. US State Department and embassy cables published by the WikiLeaks organization ("The Carter Cables")—extracts from which appear here—provide us with unique insight into how this dramatic change in Somalia's international relations came about in such a short period of time:*

From: Department of State
To: US Embassy, Mogadishu, Somalia
Date: 27/01/1977
Subject: SOVIET EXPLANATIONS TO SOMALIA CONCERNING
POSSIBLE AID TO ETHIOPIA

> . . . In a conversation with a Department [of State] officer on January 26, Somali ambassador [to Washington] Addou admitted that the [Somali Government] was gravely concerned by the growing Soviet–Ethiopian connection.[1]

---------------

From: US Embassy, Mogadishu, Somalia
To: US Secretary of State
Date: 20/02/1977
Subject: SIAD'S COMMENTS TO AMBASSADOR YOUNG

> . . . In his conversation with [US] Ambassador [to the UN, Andrew] Young, [Somali President] Siad seems to have made no concessions to US interests or sensibilities, continuing line that US is cause of nearly all major international problems. From this it follows, as Siad has told us on other occasions, that it is up to us to change [our] foreign policies generally and to make substantial, preferably financial, gesture to [Somalia] . . . before [Somalia] can consider improvement in US/Somalia relations.[2]

---------------

---

[1] Text available at https://wikileaks.org/plusd/cables/1977STATE018293_c.html (last accessed September 6, 2019).
[2] Text available at https://wikileaks.org/plusd/cables/1977MOGADI00285_c.html (last accessed September 6, 2019).

From: US Embassy, Mogadishu, Somalia
To: US Embassy, Addis Ababa, Ethiopia
Date: 10/03/1977
Subject: [Government of Somalia] REACTION TO SEELYE VISIT

> [Somali] Vice President Hussein Kulmiye Afrah called in [US] Ambassador [to Somalia, John] Loughram March 8 to say that the [Somali Government] was satisfied with results of 1–3 March visit of [US] Deputy Assistant [Secretary of State for African Affairs, Talcott] Seelye [to Mogadishu]. According to Kulmiye, President Siad told him visit had cleared the air and encouraged hope for improved bilateral relations.[3]

---------------

From: US Embassy, Mogadishu, Somalia
To: US Secretary of State
Date: 05/04/1977
Subject: THOUGHTS ON US POLICY TOWARDS [Government of Somalia]

> . . . Although [the Somali Government] is making a studied effort to portray things as unchanged, and there has been no let up . . . in rhetorical war on "imperialism," diplomatic situation has evolved strongly since Ambassador Seelye's visit one month ago. I believe that the [Somali Government] has received salutary lessons in the self-interestedness of Soviet assistance and will not return to its previous, uncritical attachment to Soviets . . . US has opportunity to improve its position in Somalia if it wishes . . . this need not mean switching horses from Ethiopia to Somalia but does mean more even-handed US approach in Horn of Africa.[4]

---------------

From: US Department of State
To: US Embassy, Mogadishu, Somalia
Date: 03/06/1977
Subject: SOMALI AMBASSADOR'S CALL ON ASSISTANT SECRETARY

> . . . [Somali] Ambassador Addou closed with a renewed request for prompt military assistance. He noted again that President Siad was

---

[3] Text available at https://wikileaks.org/plusd/cables/1977MOGADI00414_c.html (last accessed September 6, 2019).
[4] Text available at https://wikileaks.org/plusd/cables/1977MOGADI00582_c.html (last accessed September 6, 2019).

under great pressure and said an immediate favorable US response would strengthen the friendly elements in [the Somali Government].[5]

---------------

From: US Department of State
To: US Embassy, Mogadishu, Somalia
Date: 12/07/1977
Subject: SOMALIA REQUESTS US ARMS

On July 8 . . . Ambassador Addou met at his urgent request with [US] Assistant Secretary [for African Affairs, Richard] Moose. Addou reported that President Siad had been very favourably impressed by forthcoming attitude towards Somalia expressed ... by US officials, especially that of President Carter . . . Addou had accordingly been instructed to present to US a military shopping list which Addou described as "minimum needed to fill existing gaps in Somalia's defensive structure."[6]

---------------

From: US Department of State
To: US Embassy, Mogadishu, Somalia
Date: 19/07/1977
Subject: SOMALI REQUEST FOR US ARMS

Meeting with Somali Ambassador Addou on July 15, [US] Under-Secretary [of State for Political Affairs, Philip] Habib conveyed the [US] President's decision to that the US agreed in principle to respond favourably to Somalia's request for arms.

As this chapter demonstrates, though, what mattered for the states and their leaders was not simply their strategic importance. Of equal if not greater significance was their ability to creatively respond to major shifts in global politics. The Berlin Wall fell in November 1989, and the Soviet Union itself collapsed two years later. This left some authoritarian African states without a Cold War patron, and others without a card to play in dealing with Washington. A number of long-standing authoritarian leaders lost power on the back of this

---

[5] Text available at https://wikileaks.org/plusd/cables/1977STATE128517_c.html (last accessed September 6, 2019).
[6] Text available at https://wikileaks.org/plusd/cables/1977STATE161221_c.html (last accessed September 6, 2019).

international realignment, particularly since Western aid donors now felt empowered—albeit briefly—to use their aid flows to promote multiparty democracy. A combination of Soviet withdrawal from Africa, **aid conditionality**, and domestic pressure ended the authoritarian presidencies of Zambia's Kenneth Kaunda, Benin's Mathieu Kérékou, and Malawi's Hastings Banda between 1991 and 1994. Together, the three men had ruled for over a century.

In some respects, this transformation was sweeping and profound. Between 1989 and the end of the 1990s, almost all African states that were not in conflict committed themselves to holding multiparty elections of one form or another. Today, Eritrea stands out as one of the few states to have retained a **one-party state**, but it is now very much the exception. However, early hopes that the victory of the United States in the Cold War would usher in a new era of liberal democracy, and that Western pressure would lead to the emergence of a new set of political systems around the world in the American image, proved to be wide of the mark. Instead, the subsequent decades demonstrated the limits of international influence in Africa and the remarkable resilience of authoritarian governments.

As we will see, some authoritarian regimes were able to survive this pivotal moment through political savvy. Togo's Gnassingbé Eyadéma and Kenya's Daniel arap Moi bowed to pressure to end their country's one-party systems, but skillfully outmaneuvered domestic rivals to rig elections and remain in power for a further decade. The most successful and enduring, though, reframed their value to international partners in line with new global agendas around conflict resolution and economic development. The socialist-leaning governments of Mozambique and Uganda rapidly transformed themselves into pro-Washington "donor darlings," while Zaïre's Mobutu Sese Seko presented himself to Western powers as a regional force for stability and security in the aftermath of the devastating 1994 Rwandan genocide. Through a discussion of these cases, this chapter outlines the complex layers of opportunity and threat faced by authoritarian African states in engaging with the international community during, and beyond, the Cold War.

## FOREIGN AID AND THE COLD WAR: 1975–1990

Aside from Liberia and Ethiopia, every modern African state has a recent colonial experience. Even parts of contemporary Ethiopia had been held by Britain until the 1950s. These ties remain important because although the vast majority of these states gained formal independence in the middle of the last century, in reality the break with the former colonial power was rarely clear-cut. France, for example, maintained large garrisons of troops in most of its former colonies and insisted that they retain the Central/West African Franc—a currency introduced in 1945 and tied to the French Franc. Similarly, British judges continued to preside over Kenyan and Uganda courts until the 1980s, and Europe remained the primary market for African products in the years following independence. The continent's authoritarian regimes were therefore deeply embedded in the Western-dominated international system from early in their lifetimes.

The heightening of Cold War tensions between the United States and the Soviet Union during the 1960s, however, introduced a new dynamic into Africa's international relations—suddenly, there was a much larger group of international actors looking to engage with the continent, reducing the reliance of governments on the former colonial power. French assistance to Guinea, for example, was cut almost overnight after it voted for full independence from France in 1958 and rejected the opportunity to join the new "French Community" of former colonial states. Sékou Touré, Guinea's first president and leader of a one-party state from 1960, declared that his people preferred "freedom in poverty to riches in slavery." Angered by this perceived slight, departing French administrators sought to bankrupt the newly independent country by suspending all ties and even, reportedly, tearing electrical cables out of the walls of colonial buildings to take back to Paris. Far from facing international isolation and economic ruin, however, Guinea thrived because Touré was able to broker support from a new ally: the Soviet Union. A declared Marxist, Touré signed a military agreement with Moscow soon after Guinean independence and within a few years the majority of Guinean exports were finding a market behind the Iron Curtain.

In order to appreciate how this transformation occurred, it is important to recognize that the Cold War was not a traditional conflict. Its two main belligerents—the United States and the Soviet Union—could not afford to face one another directly on the battlefield; they each possessed enough nuclear weapons to annihilate each other and their allies many times over. Instead, the conflict was fought through proxy wars and the accruing of ideological allies in every region of the world. In Washington, policymakers were deeply concerned by the so-called domino theory—the idea that if one country fell to communism, so too, soon enough, would its neighbor, and that country's neighbor, and so forth. While east and southeast Asia would become the main

US regional concern in this regard, "containing" communism in Africa would also be a key priority.

Consequently, anti-communist authoritarian regimes in Africa were able to rely on sustained US support for much of the 1960s, 1970s, and 1980s—just as their communist counterparts could rely on the same from the Soviet Union, as well as several other socialist states (see Box 4.2). Playing the two sides off against one another, as the earlier Somalia example demonstrates, could be a useful strategy to "renegotiate terms" and, indeed, Touré employed this tactic himself during the mid-1970s when Soviet support began to decrease. Partly as a result, the amount that the Cold War powers spent on maintaining healthy ties with African states increased enormously during this period. Between 1960 and 1980, foreign aid to Africa grew from US$0.6 billion to nearly US$8 billion with large sums going to some of the most dictatorial regimes on the continent.[7] Mobutu's government in Zaïre, for example, received hundreds of millions of dollars in aid annually from Washington in the 1970s, while the brutal *Derg* regime in Ethiopia (see Chapter 2) commanded nearly two-thirds of Moscow's entire African aid budget by 1982.

---

**Box 4.2    From China to Cuba: The Cold War in Africa**

While support from the United States or Soviet Union was of central importance to many authoritarian African regimes during the Cold War, Washington and Moscow were not the only significant international players on the continent.

The United Kingdom and France remained particularly influential in many of their former colonies, though rarely promoted positions not held by the United States. At times, however, US policymakers themselves prioritized the containment of communism in Africa over the preferences of their European allies. In 1965, for example, the white minority regime of Ian Smith in Rhodesia—a self-governing British territory—announced a "Unilateral Declaration of Independence" from the United Kingdom. London responded by condemning this move and securing—in 1966 and 1968—UN trade sanctions against the Smith regime. In 1971,

---

[7] Data available from the World Bank. See https://data.worldbank.org/indicator/ DT.ODA.ALLD.CD?locations=ZG&name_desc=false (last accessed September 6, 2019).

however, US lawmakers passed legislation to partially exempt the United States from this embargo—fearing that an isolated Smith regime would fall to the leftist rebel movements waging guerrilla war against it.

China came to be an important supporter of a number of socialist African governments—sometimes supplementing Soviet aid, sometimes filling the vacuum created by its absence. Chinese assistance was particularly critical for the regimes of Kenneth Kaunda in Zambia and Julius Nyerere in Tanzania, both of which espoused versions of socialism which fitted well with that promoted by Beijing. This aid came primarily in the form of infrastructure—notably the construction of the TAZARA railway between 1970 and 1975 (Monson 2011). Other forms of support offered by socialist states included vocational and educational training—such as that provided by East Germany to Mozambique (Müller 2014)—and even direct military intervention. Tens of thousands of Cuban troops, for example, were dispatched to socialist Angola in 1975 to bolster the position of the newly installed leftist government. The latter was engaged in a civil war with US/South Africa–backed right-wing movements, ultimately emerging victorious in 2002.

This was not a positive development for many of those living under African authoritarian regimes. Being able to rely on external assistance—in the form of financial flows, weaponry, and military training—shielded many African leaders from needing to gain, or maintain, the support of their own people. In turn, external funding empowered vicious and covetous dictators to disregard the opinions and rights of their citizens in pursuit of whatever personal project they wished to implement, whether this was the building of an enormous palace and embezzling of billions of dollars from the state's coffers (Mobutu) or the enactment of a brutal assault on supposed counterrevolutionary forces (the *Derg*'s 1977 "Red Terror"). The international politics of the Cold War in Africa thus facilitated the curtailment of political accountability in a range of authoritarian states and provided core financing for armies and security services whose primary targets, more often than not, would be fellow citizens rather than foreign enemies. It is therefore not a coincidence that some of the most excessively violent and autocratic African political leaders flourished at the height of the Cold War. Further examples include Uganda's Idi Amin, Equatorial Guinea's

Francisco Macías Nguema, and Central African Republic's Jean-Bédel Bokassa.

These global dynamics also, however, generated fresh threats to authoritarian leaders because being an ally of one Cold War superpower attracted the enmity of the other. Uganda's Milton Obote—whose domestic policies were framed around socialism—was deposed in a 1971 military coup that is alleged to have been supported by Western powers who were concerned by his drift to the left. Similarly, Soviet-backed regimes in Angola and Mozambique during the 1970s and 1980s were forced to engage in years of civil conflict against rebel movements supported and financed by the United States and its allies. External actors could also only do so much to protect their African partners against power shifts and recalibrations at home, as the fall of Haile Selassie of Ethiopia—a long-standing US ally—revealed.

## THE FALL OF THE BERLIN WALL AND THE RISE OF POLITICAL CONDITIONALITY: 1989–1994

Navigating the Cold War was not, however, to be a permanent feature of African post-independence international relations. In November 1989, the Berlin Wall fell, signaling the refusal of Germans to accept the partition of their country into a "West," aligned with the United States, and an "East," under the indirect control of the Soviet Union. Eighteen months later, the Soviet Union itself collapsed following a series of uprisings in which people in countries such as Poland and the former Czechoslovakia rejected Soviet rule. With it went the threat of a communist world revolution that had played such a prominent role in shaping US and wider Western preoccupations and foreign policy since the 1940s. Almost overnight Western aid donors' rationales for supporting anticommunist authoritarians in Africa evaporated, removing, for many regimes, a critical source of support which had long been taken for granted. As Yoweri Museveni—who had become Ugandan president in January 1986—observed, the end of the Cold War "orphaned" many African dictators.

In Benin, a Marxist-Leninist one-party state since 1974, the unexpected withdrawal of Soviet support further destabilized the ailing regime of Mathieu Kérékou, which had mismanaged the Beninois economy over the previous two decades. Unable to rely on external support to pay civil servants and suppress increasingly radical domestic protests, Kérékou was forced to convene a "national conference" in an effort to appease his critics. The conference, which included representatives of churches, trade unions, students, and other civil society groups, declared itself sovereign, stripped Kérékou of much of his power, developed a new multiparty constitution, and held Benin's first multiparty elections since the 1970s in March 1991. Kérékou received only 32 percent of the vote in this poll, becoming the first continental African president to lose power through the ballot box. Indeed, the withdrawal of external support from many authoritarian regimes that followed the end of the Cold War empowered a range of formerly oppressed groups and civil society actors across West Africa to challenge authoritarian rule and push for democratic reform during this period. National conferences were also held in Gabon, Togo, Congo, Zaïre, and Mali between 1990 and 1993—although some regimes more skilled at subverting these processes and maintaining control of the political agenda than others (Nwajiaku 1994).

Declining aid flows were not the primary source of anxiety for most of Africa's aid-dependent authoritarian leaders, however. A more pressing concern was the rapid emergence of a consensus among the continent's leading donors that aid should now be used to promote the newly developed concept of "good governance," which usually meant reducing corruption, holding elections, and respecting human rights. Persuaded that the outcome of the Cold War had demonstrated that the Western "model" of liberal democracy was politically and economically superior,[8] senior policymakers in London, Washington, and even Paris redirected their aid policies toward the ending of one-party and one-man rule in Africa, and beyond. During the early 1990s, key Western policymakers outlined a new aid agenda that was referred to as "political conditionality." Whereas during the Cold War the key criteria for receiving aid was loyalty—a different kind of conditionality that required states to adopt a specific foreign policy but said much less about domestic policy—African governments were now told that funds would be withheld from, or suspended to, states that refused to pursue political reforms. Box 4.3 contains some of the key policy statements asserting and defending political conditionality from this period.

---

[8] Francis Fukuyama's argument that "what we may be witnessing . . . is the end point of mankind's ideological evolution and the universalization of Western liberal democracy as the final form of human government"—popularized in his 1992 book *The End of History and the Last Man* (New York: Free Press)—is perhaps the most well-known scholarly exposition of this triumphalist post–Cold War mentality.

## Box 4.3 The Era of Political Conditionality

"The United States would give preference in its grants of foreign aid to those countries which nourished democratic institutions, defended human rights and practiced multi-party politics."

Smith Hempstone, US Ambassador to Kenya,
May 1990 (Murunga 2007)

"Governments which persist with oppressive policies, corrupt management, wasteful and discredited economic systems should not expect us to support their folly with scarce aid resources which could be better used elsewhere."

Douglas Hurd, UK Foreign Secretary,
June 1990 (Robinson 1993)

"We do not conceal our expectation that true democracies with multi-partyism, free elections and respect for human rights will be established, and we will encourage developments that lead to them."

François Mitterrand, President of the French Republic,
June 1990 (IDS 1993)

"The [European] Community's response to violations of human rights will avoid penalising the population for governmental actions . . . the Community and its Member States may adjust [aid] cooperation activities with a view to ensuring that development aid benefits more directly the poorest sections of the population . . . while at the same time establishing a certain distance vis-à-vis the government."

European Council Resolution on Human Rights,
Democracy and Development, November 1991[9]

"The aid programme plays a central role in our efforts to promote good government and economic reform. . . . We withhold aid—apart from humanitarian assistance—from those who perpetuate dictatorship, who trample on human rights, who allow corruption to spread unchecked . . . it is a policy which involves both incentives and penalties, carrots and sticks."

Lynda Chalker, UK Minister of State for Overseas
Development, March 1995 (Chalker 1995)

---

[9] Full text available at http://archive.idea.int/lome/bgr_docs/resolution.html (accessed September 6, 2019).

One of the first "victims" of political conditionality was Zambia's Kenneth Kaunda. As we have seen, Kaunda was a hero of the country's independence struggle against Britain and became its first president in October 1964. He subsequently introduced a one-party state that was more inclusive and participatory than many other authoritarian regimes in Africa, but nonetheless failed to respect the political rights and civil liberties of its citizens. For example, while citizens were given a vote on the presidency, they were not allowed to select the candidate of their choice and instead were only allowed to vote "Yes" or "No" in favor of Kaunda himself. To try and ensure a "Yes" vote, the government consistently used positive symbols such as powerful birds to represent Kaunda, while picking negative or weak ones like frogs and hyenas to represent a "No" vote. But even with this kind of symbolic manipulation—which can be particularly powerful where literacy levels are low and so many voters use pictures to identify their preferred option—the government was forced to increasingly manipulate the result of these polls in the 1980s to ensure that he "won" (Figure 4.1 is an example of the ballot paper used in Zambian one-party elections between 1973 and 1988).

As set out in the last chapter, by the mid-1980s Kaunda faced growing domestic opposition as a result of the country's disastrous

| INSTRUCTIONS: | Mark one cross X only in the blank box against either YES or NO | | |
|---|---|---|---|
| QUESTION | ANSWER | SYMBOL | MARK IN THIS COLUMN |
| DO YOU WISH TO VOTE IN FAVOUR OF THE PRESIDENTIAL CANDIDATE | **YES** | | |
| **DR KENNETH DAVID KAUNDA?** | **NO** | | |

**FIGURE 4.1**   Zambian ballot paper from one-party state era.

*Source*: This is a reproduction of a Zambian ballot paper used in a one-party election created by the authors. The animal images were sourced from kbibibi - www.freepik.com.

economic performance. At the time, Zambia owed more money to international creditors relative to its national wealth than almost any other country in the world, which meant that it could not meet the demands of powerful trade union groups. Indeed, the influence of organized labor meant that Kaunda found himself stuck between a rock and a particularly hard place: he needed international financial assistance to survive, but the restrictive policies demanded by the International Monetary Fund and the World Bank were so unpopular that they mobilized Zambians against him. This meant that while losing international support threatened to bankrupt his regime, gaining it risked triggering trade-union disapproval and mass protests.

Ultimately, growing popular frustration in the late 1980s consolidated into the emergence of a broad coalition for change that came to be known as the Movement for Multi-party Democracy (MMD). In turn, the combination of burgeoning support for the MMD and the reluctance of international donors to fund his poorly performing government forced Kaunda to abandon the one-party state. However, his early hope that it might be possible to use political reforms to relegitimize his UNIP regime and hence regain control of the political agenda proved to be unrealistic. When opposition parties were legalized in 1990, the MMD transformed itself from a civil society alliance into an effective political machine and shrewdly selected Frederick Chiluba, a former Chairman of the Zambia Congress of Trade Unions, to be its presidential candidate. Backed by both trade union infrastructure and business leaders, Chiluba went on to comprehensively defeat Kaunda, who secured only 24 percent of the vote—one of the worst performances of any incumbent president in African history.

Perhaps the most dramatic examples of political conditionality— cited at the time by scholars as evidence that conditionality "worked"— took place in Malawi and Kenya between 1991 and 1994. Between them, Kenya's Daniel arap Moi and Malawi's Hastings Kamuzu Banda and their Kenyan African National Union and Malawi Congress Party had held power for nearly sixty years and by the early 1990s both were being increasingly criticized for their harsh treatment of domestic opponents. Particularly controversial episodes included the suspicious death of Kenyan foreign minister Robert Ouko in February 1990 (widely viewed as a murder and reportedly carried out in one of Moi's residences) and an incident in which Malawian police open fired on striking textile factory workers in May 1992.

In tense "Consultative Group" meetings held by donors and recipient governments in 1991 (Kenya) and 1992 (Malawi), donors announced their decision to suspend all nonhumanitarian aid to the two countries until significant progress on political liberalization was made. Both regimes swiftly acceded to these demands, with multiparty elections held in Kenya in December 1992 and in Malawi in May 1994. Following in Kaunda's footsteps, Banda became the third African independence struggle hero-turned-autocrat to be rejected by the electorate following the reintroduction of multiparty politics, losing power to opposition candidate Bakili Muluzi.

It is important, however, not to overstate the significance of the role that international actors played during this period. International pressure clearly triggered a political change in Kenya that might not have happened otherwise—in 1991, Moi had promised the country would not see multiparty politics for "a hundred years"—but it did not lead to a smooth process of democratization. Instead, Moi set about using a range of authoritarian strategies to retain control, including censorship, political violence, and divide-and-rule strategies that fragmented the opposition. As we shall see in the next chapter, these efforts were successful: Moi won poor-quality elections in 1992 and 1997 and only stepped down in 2002, at the grand age of seventy-eight, because he had exhausted presidential term limits. Donors could use aid to alter the formal systems of government in authoritarian states, therefore, but had limited leverage over the way that the rules of the game were implemented in practice.

Moreover, the high salience of international interventions in the early 1990s should not cause us to overlook the important role that domestic civil society and opposition groups played during this period. Political conditionality helped to destabilize authoritarian rulers and provide critical space for opposition voices to be heard, but many brave Africans had been risking their livelihoods and their lives to resist repression for decades. Indeed, the next twenty years would demonstrate that the fate of these political processes, and whether they led to genuine democracy or just the "rebranding" of authoritarian rule, depended more on the strength, unity, and energy of the domestic forces pushing for change than the actions of Western donors.

## AUTHORITARIAN SURVIVAL AND INTERNATIONAL POLITICS: 1990–2005

For many African authoritarians, therefore, the end of the Cold War represented a major watershed and a profound, sometimes fatal, disruption to the long-standing strategies of **regime maintenance** they had developed. However, in some cases authoritarian leaders were able to survive this challenge by manipulating or subverting the supposedly democratic structures they had been forced to establish. Others successfully reinvented themselves as democrats: in Nigeria, for example, two former military dictators were subsequently elected as "democratic" presidents: Olusegun Obasanjo (military leader 1976–1978; democratically elected president 1999–2007) and Muhammadu Buhari (1983–1985; 2015–). Even Kérékou returned to power this way in Benin's 1996 election, after making a very public plea for forgiveness for the abuses undertaken in his name (see Box 4.4).

---

**Box 4.4   The "Afterlives" of African Authoritarians—And Their Parties**

Prior to the 1990s, few authoritarian African leaders left office voluntarily or enjoyed any form of retirement. Presidents Léopold Senghor of Senegal and Julius Nyerere of Tanzania—who stepped down as leaders of their countries in 1980 and 1985, respectively—are the exceptions that prove the rule. This was partly because losing power placed leaders at great risk. The African military rulers who came to power across the continent during the 1970s were rarely prepared to allow their authoritarian predecessors to survive. Ethiopia's Haile Selassie, as described in Chapter 2, was murdered in 1975 by the military *junta* which overthrew him. President François Tombalbaye of Chad met the same fate (in April 1975), as did President Francisco Macías Nguema of Equatorial Guinea (1979), President William Tolbert of Liberia (1980), and many others.

Losing power has not, however, meant losing life for all of Africa's authoritarian leaders. Indeed, deposed dictators have become an increasingly commonplace feature of African politics and international relations since the end of the Cold War. This is in part the consequence of the political openings that occurred in many African states during the 1990s. The advent of multiparty democracy meant that authoritarian leaders could not only lose power through elections—as Hastings Banda of Malawi did in 1994—but also *regain* power through the same mechanism, as occurred in Benin in 1996 and Nigeria in 1999 and 2015.

However, this period also saw the emergence of a new set of problems for defeated authoritarians as a result of the growing reach of continental and global international justice mechanisms from the early 2000s onward—following years of advocacy and lobbying by

African civil society coalitions—which posed a new threat to leaders that had committed human rights abuses. The risk of being brought before an international court and sentenced to life imprisonment if they are overthrown incentivized several African presidents to come to an arrangement with domestic opponents, or to flee into exile, when their position has been imperiled. President Robert Mugabe of Zimbabwe, for example, negotiated a comfortable post-presidency retirement in 2017 with those who forced him to resign. By contrast, President Laurent Gbagbo of Côte d'Ivoire refused to back down after losing a 2010 election and suffered the consequences when he was eventually apprehended, arrested, and charged with crimes against humanity by the International Criminal Court—although the trial later collapsed.

Partly as a result of these challenges, many African authoritarians coming to the end of their time in power have been attracted to the idea of exile to a safe third-country where they can be assured of their safety and immunity from prosecution for crimes committed while in office. Former dictators in exile have often selected authoritarian states as their hosts, knowing that these countries are less likely to open themselves up to global justice systems. Thus, Mengistu Hailemariam of Ethiopia fled to Zimbabwe in 1991, and The Gambia's Yahya Jammeh went to Equatorial Guinea in 2017. Exile has also provided the opportunity for some authoritarian leaders to plot a return to power, as Idi Amin and Milton Obote of Uganda both did—ultimately unsuccessfully—from Saudi Arabia and Kenya, respectively, during the 1980s.

For their part, the political parties of authoritarian leaders have rarely survived the removal, or retirement, of these leaders themselves (Tanzania's Chama Cha Mapinduzi is an important exception). Hastings Banda's Malawi Congress Party, for example, has continued to perform well in parliamentary elections since Banda's departure but has never regained the presidency. In Kenya, Uganda, and Zambia, the political backbones of the one-party state—the Kenya African National Union, Uganda People's Congress, and United National Independence Party, respectively—are now marginal political players; none has more than ten seats in their country's legislature at the time of writing. The fate of these parties underlines how central certain "big men" were to the longevity of their political movements, and also demonstrates how fragile many of these political structures became when forced to operate in a multiparty context—despite appearances to the contrary.

The most durable authoritarian regimes, however, prevailed by viewing the changed international situation as an opportunity, rather than a threat. Major Western powers were no longer concerned about the spread of communism, but this did not mean that they no longer had any priorities in Africa. In 1993, a US peacekeeping intervention in Somalia ended disastrously, with the bodies of dead US soldiers dragged through the streets of Mogadishu by victorious rebels. A year later the international community, and the United States in particular, was vilified for its inaction in the face of genocide in Rwanda. Western policymakers were therefore keen to find a way to promote stability in the continent without having to become directly involved. Zaïre's Mobutu Sese Seko, who had been pressured by donors and domestic forces into forming a coalition government in 1991, presented himself to the United States as a tried-and-tested regional sheriff and a reliable guarantor of stability in a deeply unpredictable part of Africa. He also reassured French politicians that he would protect France's interests in the region after Anglophone rebels took power in French-speaking Rwanda. Restored to favor in Paris and Washington, Mobutu—one of the most repressive figures in recent African history—was able not only to secure sufficient resources to remain in office for several years but also, for a short while, to strengthen his grip on power.

In Mozambique and Uganda, leftist, revolutionary regimes attempted a different kind of transformation, presenting themselves as obedient implementers of World Bank–designed economic development programs in an effort to broker the opportunities presented by the new international order. Though many of Museveni's National Resistance Movement comrades had been inspired by Marx, Lenin, and Mao Zedong of China, the Ugandan leader had few qualms about offering his country to Western aid donors as a laboratory for liberal economic development reforms, even defending free market economics at the UN General Assembly. This strategy went one step further than Mobutu's in terms of ensuring consistent international support, because governments in Kampala and Maputo were now implementing *donor* recommendations, and so their fate became particularly important to the international community as it had the potential to validate or refute state-of-the-art donor wisdom. Policymakers in London and Washington therefore sought to give their experiments in Mozambique and Uganda the best possible chance of success by backing them financially. They also moderated their criticisms of the increasingly authoritarian approaches to governance occurring in the two countries, afraid that cutting off aid or demanding further political reforms might jeopardize "their" success stories (Hauser 1999).

## CONCLUSION: DOES THE TAIL WAG THE DOG?

The 9/11 al-Qaeda terrorist attacks on the United States in 2001, and President George W. Bush's subsequent declaration of a "Global War on Terrorism," provided further opportunities for Africa's authoritarian states to leverage international policy agendas in their favor. It is little coincidence that the five African states which supported the 2003 US-led Iraq War—Angola, Eritrea, Ethiopia, Rwanda, and Uganda—were, and are, also among the continent's most authoritarian states. By making themselves core US allies at a time of conflict, the governments of these countries hoped to make themselves indispensable to American leaders, and to mute criticism of their refusal to democratize—reviving a classic Cold War strategy.

As this chapter has shown, though, the international system has been at best a double-edged sword for Africa's authoritarian regimes. Very few have been able to survive by cutting themselves off from international networks, and while some have been able to sustain their rule by forming partnerships with foreign governments, none have been able to consistently rely upon external support. Thus, while scholars such as Jean-François Bayart have underscored how uniquely intertwined domestic and international politics have been since the colonial era, arguing that African governments have survived by manipulating this relationship to their own advantage (Bayart 2000), leaders have often been left disappointed when foreign assistance dries up. During an interview with one of the authors in April 2007, for example, one of the closest confidantes of Hastings Banda noted that the Malawian president had felt "deeply betrayed" in 1992 when donors "turned against him."[10] Banda had been a staunch US and UK partner during the Cold War and the only African leader to maintain diplomatic ties with apartheid South Africa (a British ally); he had assumed—wrongly—that this loyalty would be rewarded in the post–Cold War era.

---

[10] Jonathan Fisher interview with Cecilia Kadzamira, Former Official Hostess of Malawi, by telephone, April 2007.

Authoritarian regimes such as Rwanda's Rwandan Patriotic Front have, by contrast, been more pragmatic and calculating in their engagement with the international system. Viewing Western donors as "often predatory, and even abusive, in nature" (2015), the government of Paul Kagame has willingly accepted vast amounts of aid to support its developmental and state-building activities since 1994 without ever becoming dependent on it. Under this approach, policymakers in ministries and government agencies are expected to seek and use aid money effectively, while being constantly reminded by their superiors that donors are ultimately self-interested and unreliable.

As we shall see in greater detail in the next two chapters, countries such as Rwanda were empowered to adopt more critical approaches to Western donors, in part, by the shifting balance of power within the international community. Increasingly, Western donors are being eclipsed by different players that engage with the continent in a different way. Most notably, China and the Gulf States have come to represent a critical alternative source of external assistance to authoritarian regimes, including in Zimbabwe, Sudan, and Eritrea. Unlike their Western counterparts, these states do not even pay lip service to the notion of promoting democracy, creating fresh opportunities for the continent's authoritarian regimes.

## REFERENCES

Bayart, Jean-François. "Africa in the World: A History of Extraversion." *African Affairs* 99, no. 935 (2000): 217–67.

Chalker, Lynda. "Britain and Africa: Support for Peaceful Change." Speech delivered at Chatham House, London, March 2, 1995.

"The Emergence of the "Good Government" Agenda: Some Milestones." *IDS Bulletin* 24, no. 1 (1993): 7–8.

Hauser, Ellen. "Ugandan Relations with Western Donors in the 1990s: What Impact on Democratisation?." *The Journal of Modern African Studies* 37, no. 4 (1999): 621–41.

Monson, Jamie. *Africa's Freedom Railway: How a Chinese Development Project Changed Lives and Livelihoods in Tanzania*. Bloomington: Indiana University Press, 2011.

Müller, Tanja R. *Legacies of Socialist Solidarity: East Germany in Mozambique*. New York: Lexington Books, 2014.

Murunga, Godwin. "The State, Its Reform, and the Question of Legitimacy in Kenya." In *Beyond State Failure and Collapse: Making the State Relevant in Africa*, edited by George Klay Kieh Jr. New York: Lexington Books, 2007.

Nwajiaku, Kathryn. "The National Conferences in Benin and Togo." *Journal of Modern African Studies* 32, no. 3 (1994): 429–47.

Robinson, Mark. "Will Political Conditionality Work?" *IDS Bulletin* 24, no. 1 (1993): 58–66.

## SUGGESTED READINGS

Bratton, Michael, and Nicholas van de Walle. *Democratic Experiments in Africa: Regime Transitions in Comparative Perspective.* Cambridge: Cambridge University Press, 1997.

Brautigam, Deborah. *The Dragon's Gift: The Real Story of China in Africa.* Oxford: Oxford University Press, 2009.

Clapham, Christopher. *Africa and the International System: The Politics of State Survival.* Cambridge: Cambridge University Press, 1996.

Gebru, Tareke. *The Ethiopian Revolution: War in the Horn of Africa.* New Haven, CT: Yale University Press, 2013.

Hempstone, Smith. *Rogue Ambassador: An African Memoir.* Sewanee, TN: University of the South Press, 1997.

Khadiagala, Gilbert, and Terrence Lyons, eds. *African Foreign Policies: Power and Process.* Lynne Rienner, 2001.

Lancaster, Carol. *Foreign Aid: Diplomacy, Development, Domestic Politics.* Chicago: University of Chicago Press, 2006.

McNulty, Mel. "The Collapse of Zaïre: Implosion, Revolution or External Sabotage?" *Journal of Modern African Studies* 37, no. 1 (1999): 53–82.

Schmidt, Elizabeth. *Foreign Intervention in Africa: From the Cold War to the War on Terror.* Cambridge: Cambridge University Press, 2013.

Schmidt, Elizabeth. *Foreign Intervention in Africa after the Cold War.* Athens: Ohio University Press, 2018.

# Authoritarian Rule 2.0

*Multiparty Africa and the Struggle for
Democracy, 1995–2010*

On March 1, 1992, lines of people formed outside of polling stations
in Cameroon as citizens queued up to exercise their democratic rights
in the first multiparty election to be held in the country since the 1960s.
Under President Paul Biya, who first came to power in 1982, Cameroon
had held a series of one-party elections in which opposition parties
were not allowed to compete. The reintroduction of competitive elections initially generated great excitement and hope among civil society
groups and critics of the government, who saw this democratic open-
ing as an opportunity to elect leaders who would be more responsive to
the needs of their people. But their dreams were soon crushed. When-
ever the government felt that it might lose overall political control, it
clamped down through a combination of censorship and intimidation,
while protests against Biya's government "were violently put down
by the security forces, resulting in hundreds of arrests and deaths"
(Cheeseman 2015: 149).

Any hope that the issues witnessed in 1992 would turn out to be
a short-term "teething problem" quickly evaporated as elections held
in 1997 and 2004 repeated the same combination of repression and
electoral fraud. According to the United Nations Committee Against

Torture, the government's security forces systematically used torture against those held in detention, including pro-democracy activists. The situation had improved little by 2009, when Amnesty International reported that "The authorities have repeatedly used violence, arbitrary arrests and unlawful detentions to prevent opposition political parties and political activists from holding public or private meetings."

In addition to violence, Biya made sure that he would not lose power by manipulating the voting and counting process. Robert Jackson, the US Ambassador to Cameroon in 2011, noted that "on election day, mission observers noted inconsistencies and irregularities in and between almost all polling stations." Partly as a result, Biya won a series of landslide victories, taking over 70 percent of the vote in 1997, 2004, and 2011. This run of illegitimate victories was extended in October 2018, when Biya—now eighty-five—was returned to power for the seventh time. Along with human rights violations against the English-speaking minority, the election was marked by widespread accusations of electoral manipulation. Although twenty-five complaints were lodged by candidates and voters calling for the elections to be annulled, they were all dismissed by the electoral commission. This was not a surprise: the president appoints all of its members. Having officially won 71 percent of the vote, it is becoming increasingly obvious that Biya intends to be a "life president." The country's supposed "second liberation"—the first being freedom from colonial rule—proved to be a false dawn.

Cameroon's experience with elections has been particularly bleak, but is not unique, either in terms of the timing of the reintroduction of multiparty elections or in the way that the government subsequently manipulated them.

By the 1990s, many of the conditions that had sustained authoritarian rule in the 1970s and 1980s had changed. As we saw in Chapter 3, throughout the 1970s and 1980s, many one-party states and military regimes experienced economic stagnation or decline. This made it more difficult to co-opt support and meant that a range of African governments became increasingly dependent on external—primarily Western—financial support to fund their budgets. At the same time, generational change on the continent created new challenges. The young people becoming politically active from the mid-1980s onward had not been alive during the anticolonial struggle and were often less willing to support a government on the basis of its former "nationalist" credentials. Instead, they wanted jobs and economic opportunities—something that their governments increasingly struggled to provide.

The international changes described in the last chapter—the end of the Cold War and the greater interest of a number of Western countries in promoting multiparty democracy abroad—were significant because they occurred in this context. In other words, the pressure that the United Kingdom and the United States placed on African states to open up their political systems had, in some instances, dramatic effects because the conditions on the ground were already ripe for political change. In many cases, in fact, African civil society coalitions had been pushing for reform for years—fighting authoritarian systems bankrolled by the same Western states who now became their allies.

The economic dependence of many African governments on foreign loans made them more susceptible to international pressure. At the same time, growing international condemnation of human rights abuses made it harder for authoritarian leaders to simply repress their opponents, creating new space for opposition leaders and civil society groups to mobilize for change. It is the combination and interaction of all of these domestic and international changes that helps to explain why so many leaders felt compelled to legalize opposition parties and introduce multiparty elections in the early 1990s.

In the euphoria of the time, these political openings were often interpreted as a moment of rebirth that would generate an opportunity for African people to forge new democratic futures. But as in Cameroon, many of these hopes were dashed. Authoritarianism did not simply wither and die. Instead, authoritarian leaders adopted new strategies that enabled them to retain support both at home and abroad, and hence stay in power, and new ways to rig the system to their own advantage. As we have already discussed, this was easier to do when foreign governments were willing to sacrifice democracy for other goals such as security, or when natural resource wealth cushioned the blow of economic decline.

This chapter looks at two other developments that enabled authoritarian leaders to recast and legitimate their governments for a new political era. First, regimes that had previously sought to resist holding elections refocused their efforts on how to control and manipulate them. With the notable exception of Eritrea, the one-party states of the 1980s gave way to a set of multiparty systems in which governments allowed opposition parties to compete, but usually at a great disadvantage. By ensuring that their rivals lacked resources, press coverage, and equal treatment under the law, many ruling parties were able to undermine the impact of the transition to multiparty politics, giving rise to "elections without change."

In this context, holding elections could, paradoxically, actually make authoritarian leaders stronger (Cheeseman and Klaas 2018). By conforming to democratic norms and discourses, and permitting multipartyism, governments could claim international respectability and legitimacy. By rigging these polls, they could ensure that they would not actually lose power. Pulling off this particular trick was not possible, however, if governments routinely committed the kind of widespread human rights abuses that would trigger condemnation from organizations such as Amnesty International and undermine their reputation in the international media. The 1990s therefore saw the evolution of more subtle forms of repression and election rigging that were often just as effective as those used in the 1980s, but much harder to detect.

Second, as we have already seen in the case of Uganda, the continent's more forward-thinking authoritarian rulers set about legitimizing their governments by managing their economies particularly well, while reducing corruption and forming **developmental** partnerships with European and North American aid agencies. In addition to generating the revenue needed to provide services and co-opt support, this had the benefit of building a positive narrative that could be used to package authoritarian regimes and sell them to the world. In a continent still suffering from high levels of poverty and unemployment, leaders able to deliver public services and reduce corruption could gain domestic and international support, even if they had limited democratic credentials.

Taken together, these changes enabled some of Africa's authoritarian leaders to change their image from anachronistic relics of the past to forces for progress and innovation. In the process, they also changed the contours of the debate. Whereas authoritarian rule had been seen by many as a problem in the late 1980s—something to be bemoaned and transformed if at all possible—in the 2000s it became possible to argue that authoritarian development might have advantages, and even be preferable. Along with the global rise of China—a country that had grown in economic and political power under an authoritarian one-party state—this generated a serious challenge to Western political and economic values.

In a return to the language of the 1960s, a new generation of African leaders and intellectuals began to argue that unity was necessary for development, and that Western models might not be suitable in the African context. However, while these arguments are alluring, and resonated with many Africans who were frustrated by the continued implication that Western political systems were inherently superior, there is little evidence that authoritarian states really do outperform their democratic counterparts.

## ELECTORAL AUTHORITARIANISM

Simply holding multiparty elections does not make a county a democracy. Instead, a wider set of civil liberties is required to enable citizens to express themselves freely, join civil society groups, and move around the country. Limits on the abuse of power are also important, to prevent the government from repressing critics and using its control over the state to gain an unfair political advantage. While the exact definition of democracy is controversial, and different writers on the topic would emphasize different rights and freedoms as the most important, there is one thing that most researchers agree on: elections do not equal democracy.

Indeed, elections on their own can be very weak and vulnerable if they do not take place in the context of a supportive set of democratic institutions. For example, if the media is not free to report on the government's failings and the opposition's successes, voters may not have the information they need to make an informed decision. Even if they do, they may feel too intimidated to actually go to the polls if they fear that opposition supporters will be the targets for violence and abuse. Moreover, even if these strategies fail and citizens do cast their ballots for an opposition leader, the ruling party may still win if the electoral commission is not independent and can be persuaded to fix the result at the counting stage.

In the absence of these checks and balances, elections can be relatively easy to rig. Authoritarian leaders in Africa learned this lesson quickly and to great effect in the 1990s. Initially, it looked like things might turn out very differently. Two of the earliest elections to be held in the 1990s, in Benin and Zambia in 1991, resulted in comprehensive defeats for the government. However, while these processes inspired opposition parties to believe that change was possible, they also alerted African leaders to the potential danger that elections posed to their hold on power. If any of the continent's presidents and prime ministers were complacent about the challenge posed by elections before the fall of Presidents Kérékou and Kaunda, they were not afterward.

The methods that have been deployed to manipulate elections in Africa are too numerous to be listed here, but some of the main strategies are listed in Table 5.1. It is important to note that this list only includes illegitimate strategies; that is, it only features those tactics that would normally be considered to be undemocratic and are typically against the law in African states. Governments also enjoy a range of legitimate benefits, such as the ability to determine

**TABLE 5.1**    The African "Menu of Manipulation"

| | |
|---|---|
| Strategies used to manipulate elections[1] include but are not limited to: | |
| Exclusion | Excluding rival candidates from the election, often on the basis of the dubious claim that they or their parents were born outside of the country and so they are not eligible. |
| Gerrymandering | Manipulating the distribution of electoral constituencies so that ruling party legislators need to receive fewer votes to win their seats. |
| Vote buying | Offering voters bribes in the form of cash or small gifts in return for their vote, often through intermediaries such as traditional leaders. |
| Propaganda | Denying opposition leaders access to the media while generating fake news stories—including digitally faking documents and evidence—to make the opposition look worse and the government look better. |
| Divide and rule | Generating an atmosphere of intimidation to mobilize ruling party supporters and frighten rivals, playing on intercommunal rivalries and in some cases using violence to demobilize opposition voters. |
| Inflating the vote | Registering more people to vote than really exist so that party supporters or leaders can illegitimately vote on their behalf. |
| Rigging the count | Subtracting votes from the total for opposition candidates, or adding them to the president's total, to secure the desired result. |

government policy, to manage the economy in a way that generates a boom around the election date, to set the news agenda through the greater press coverage typically (but not always) given to the ruling party, and so on. While in some ways this is unfair to opposition parties in the sense that it puts them at a disadvantage, these benefits are present in most democracies and, more important, are within the rules.

The combined effect of this range of strategies is extremely powerful. Consider the Kenyan election of 1992. Following the ultimatum from international donors described in the last chapter, president Daniel arap Moi begrudgingly agreed to legalize opposition parties and arrange elections. However, he had no intention of losing power. Instead, Moi calculated that he was more likely to be able to retain

[1] Source: Based on Andreas Schedler, "The Menu of Manipulation," *Journal of Democracy* 13, no. 2 (2002): 36–50.

power by agreeing to hold elections quickly than by delaying the inevitable until he was in a much weaker economic and political position.

His regime could, for example, have limped on without international financial support. Indeed, this was what many hardliners in his own party demanded. Donor funding was less significant to the Kenyan treasury than many of its African counterparts and the country could have sustained its budget for some time in the absence of external assistance. But at that point, Moi would have been out of resources and out of options.

By agreeing relatively quickly to hold multiparty elections, Moi ensured that he could contest them from a position of strength. On the one hand, earlier polls ensured that his government did not run down its income and remaining domestic support. On the other hand, creating the impression that he was engaged in a process of democratic reform enabled Moi to secure further international financial assistance. In turn, money that was supposed to be spent on economic development was diverted to fund the president's election campaign (Brown 2001).

With these resources, the ruling party was able to comprehensively outspend its rivals. But Moi did not rely on this alone. His government also used the full range of the menu of manipulation. The security forces were used to intimidate opposition supporters, and opposition leaders such as Kenneth Matiba were arrested and submitted to a terrible ordeal, including detention without charge and, in some cases, torture. At the same time, the government's tight control over the media was used to pump out pro-Moi propaganda, while state officials and vehicles were used to mobilize support.

These tactics were supplemented by the use of a clever divide-and-rule strategy that had serious long-term consequences for national stability. As in most African countries, Kenya is highly ethnically diverse, with no one community making up more than a quarter of the overall population. Reflecting the legacy of colonial rule described in Chapter 1 and the divide-and-rule politics discussed in Chapter 2, the political salience of these identities meant that leaders needed to put together coalitions of different big men and their ethnic communities in order to win office. Consequently, one of the most effective ways to stay in power is to undermine the potential for an opposition alliance between different leaders and communities.

In the Kenyan context, this strategy had two different elements. The first was that the government encouraged a split within the main opposition movement, the Forum for the Restoration of Democracy (FORD). In the early 1990s, FORD had two main leaders: Matiba, a prominent figure in the Kikuyu community, and Oginga Odinga, the dominant force within the Luo ethnic group. By secretly planting government agents within FORD to exacerbate tensions between Matiba and Odinga, Moi encouraged a divisive struggle over the question of who would be the movement's presidential candidate. Once the rivalry between the two leaders had effectively fragmented FORD into two factions, the government—which had previously been reluctant to recognize any opposition parties—quickly approved the registration of two new ones: FORD-Asili led by Matiba, and FORD-Kenya under Odinga (Throup and Hornsby 1998). The creation of two new parties out of what had been one pro-democracy movement effectively split the opposition vote down the middle.

The second strategy that the regime employed was to deploy militias to attack communities that were expected to support opposition leaders because they shared the same identity, heightening ethnic tensions. By using shadowy militia groups—gangs of armed citizens—rather than the state security forces, the government hoped to escape domestic and international criticism for these human rights abuses. While sending in the army or police to commit the violence would have made it clear who was to blame, the use of shadowy gangs made it possible to argue that ethnic clashes were not the responsibility of the government, and instead represented the natural by-product of holding competitive elections in a divided society. Through tactics such as this, Moi hoped to generate an atmosphere of fear in which opposition supporters would be too scared to go to the polls, while ruling party voters would feel compelled to turn up.

In the end, these strategies proved to be highly successful, enabling the president to win elections in 1992 and 1997 against a deeply divided opposition. As a result, it was not the reintroduction of multiparty politics that ended Moi's time in office, but presidential term limits. In 2002, having fulfilled the maximum two terms in office set out in the new constitutional arrangements, Moi stood down having never lost an election.

Although some of the precise features of the Kenyan story are distinctive, Moi laid down a blueprint that many other leaders subsequently followed. Consequently, when sitting African presidents contested elections during this period, they won eight times out of ten (Cheeseman 2010). As a result, the reintroduction of multiparty politics often failed to generate far-reaching political change. Instead, many authoritarian leaders proved able to manipulate elections to keep themselves in power and—as was the case with Moi—to actually strengthen their position.

In this way, authoritarian leaders were able to transform their political systems by making them more acceptable for a new international era. In addition to the greater access to funds that holding elections facilitated, the ability of authoritarian leaders to market their countries as democratic states was extremely valuable, because it boosted their legitimacy and obscured the illegitimate strategies that were actually being used to sustain their rule. Through this process, the structure and legitimizing discourse of authoritarian Africa was transformed.

Today, the most successful authoritarian leaders on the continent retain power by manipulating elections rather than by refusing to hold them at all.

## DEVELOPMENTAL AUTHORITARIANISM

The second big change in the nature of African authoritarianism has come in the management of the economy. After a long period of decline in the 1980s, some of the most authoritarian states holding elections have sought to bolster their legitimacy by reducing poverty and promoting economic growth. Of course, this was always one of the main promises of authoritarian governments in Africa, but as we saw in Chapter 3, it was rarely realized in the 1980s, when the fastest growing states on the continent were the democracies of Botswana and Mauritius.

One of the noticeable shifts in the 1990s and the 2000s is that it is now authoritarian states that can claim this crown. In particular, Ethiopia and Rwanda have often been identified as two of the continent's best performing countries, whether it comes to the ability of governments to control corruption or inspire economic activity. This is part of a broader global trend that Roberto Foa (2018) has described as "authoritarian resurgence," in which undemocratic political systems have begun to perform better on key indicators such as providing infrastructure and improving state capacity.

Consider, for example, the world's fastest growing economies in 2017 (see Figure 5.1). Of the top 10, only India is usually rated as a full democracy. The remaining states are electoral authoritarian systems or, in the case of Laos, one-party states that do not hold multiparty elections at all. In line with this broad pattern, while the three African states to make it into the top 10—Djibouti, Ethiopia, and Tanzania—all hold elections, they do so in political systems that actively discriminate against the opposition and were ranked as either Partly Free (Tanzania) or Not Free (Djibouti and Ethiopia) that year by Freedom House.

**FIGURE 5.1**   The world's fastest growing economies in 2017.
*Source*: World Bank (2017).[2]

Significantly, in none of these three countries has the ruling party ever lost power through the ballot box.

The Rwandan model of development has been particularly praised, in part because the country's economic success appeared so unlikely. In 1994, when the forces of Paul Kagame's Rwandan Patriotic Front (RPF) took control following an invasion from Uganda that had begun in 1990, the country faced an incredible set of challenges.

The previous four years had witnesses some of the most shocking and saddening moments in African history. Under pressure to reform, and in the context of the efforts of the RPF to overthrow his regime, the country's long-term president, Juvénal Habyarimana, had agreed to replace his one-party state with a multiparty political system in 1991. However, hardline extremists within Habyarimana's government feared that political liberalization would undermine their hold on power. One of their main concerns was that members of the minority Tutsi community, which made up around 10 percent of the total population, would form an alliance with disgruntled members of the majority Hutu community, and so defeat the government.

In an effort to play divide-and-rule politics and prevent such a coalition from forming, Hutu extremists hatched an alternative plan that rested on demonizing the Tutsi community. One way of doing this was to link all Tutsis to the RPF invasion in order to brand them as enemies of the state. This approach deliberately played on a history of interethnic tension rooted in the divisive impact of Belgian colonial rule (see Chapter 1) and featured a range of tactics, including disseminating hate-speech on the radio and mobilizing a radical Hutu militia known as the *Interahamwe*. These actions collectively represented

---

[2] For this and more economic data, go to https://data.worldbank.org.

a concerted effort to create a situation in which it would be possible to retain power by exterminating the country's Tutsi community (Des Forges et al. 1999).

In 1994, when a plane carrying Habyarimana and the Burundian president, Cyprien Ntaryamira, was shot down over Kigali, the extremist elements of the government used the incident as a pretext for genocide. Blaming Tutsi forces for the assassination of the two Hutu leaders, the security forces and the *Interhamwe* began the mass murder of those deemed to be enemies of the state, triggering a period of ethnic cleansing that is estimated to have killed over 800,000 Tutsi, and thousands of Hutus who refused to take part. The wave of death was only brought to an end when RPF forces took control of Kigali, overthrowing the genocidal regime.

Now in power, the RPF government faced a number of major challenges at the same time. As a Tutsi leader in charge of a majority Hutu country, Kagame had to ensure political stability and avoid a repeat of the ethnic conflict that had torn Rwanda apart. At the same time, the RPF needed to rebuild the state and its infrastructure, constructing a new system of government. Moreover, all of this had to be done in an extremely difficult economic context, because the regime also inherited a broken economy that, because of the country's small size and recent experience of conflict, did not represent an attractive investment opportunity for foreign businesses.

The new president responded to these challenges by establishing a political and economic system designed to maintain exceptionally tight control of the state. This strategy had three main elements. First, while multiparty elections have been held, any candidates who would seriously challenge Kagame were not allowed to stand, ensuring that he has consistently won landslide victories. Second, the president asserted his personal authority over both the political system and the state bureaucracy, enforcing a clamp down on corruption and driving through his own vision of development. Third, instead of waiting for foreign investors to set up new businesses, or for free market competition to organically inspire growth, the government kick-started the economy by establishing business and investment groups that were effectively owned by the ruling party and do its bidding.

This development approach had important political and economic implications. On the economic side, the government used companies such as Tri-Star Investments to direct state resources into the parts of the economy that it believed were most important for national reconstruction and represented the best bet when it came to increasing economic growth. By channeling funds into key areas such as the mobile phone sector, and doing so effectively, the government was able to provide essential services to its citizens, generate the kind of infrastructure that would support business activity, and make a profit. In turn, the revenues generated by these ventures could then be ploughed back into additional services and further investments, boosting other parts of the economy (Booth and Golooba-Mutebi 2012).

Along with the careful management of agriculture and the provision of extremely high volumes of foreign aid by a number of Western states—many of whom were embarrassed that they had not done more to prevent the genocide—this strategy proved to be highly effective. Between 2001 and 2013, the economy grew around 8 percent per year, while the proportion of people living below the poverty line fell from 57 percent in 2005 to 45 percent in 2010 – although these figures are contested by critics who allege that the government manipulates them. The government also secured significant improvements in life expectancy and literacy.

On the political side, the RPF's economic model helped to consolidate the ruling party's dominance. By placing so much of the economy under the control of the government, the RPF enhanced its power because the party could decide who was and was not allowed to establish a successful enterprise. As a result, individuals have a strong incentive to form an alliance with the RPF whether they support its policies or not. Along with the repressive measures implemented by President Kagame, this system has helped to maintain his government's stranglehold over the political system.

At the same time, the country's economic growth has enabled Kagame to legitimate his government on the basis of the development that it has provided. In a context in which many more democratic states have struggled to reduce poverty and promote economic expansion, the RPF regime can point to its achievements in this area in order to deflect criticism of the government's poor human rights record. In particular, the Kagame government has been accused of committing a possible genocide itself, when, having taken control of Rwanda, its troops crossed the border into the Democratic Republic of Congo in pursuit of those who had orchestrated the killing of Tutsis.

The ability of the Rwandan government to use political stability and development to justify authoritarian rule is reminiscent of the focus on "unity" discussed in previous chapters. Although Rwanda is perhaps the best example of this phenomena, it is not alone—authoritarian leaders in countries such as Ethiopia and Uganda have used similar strategies to legitimize their political systems. In Uganda, for example, President Yoweri Museveni was often said to be one of the "new breed" of leaders on the continent, along with Kagame and

Ethiopia's late prime minister, Meles Zenawi. As we saw in the last chapter, this generated considerable benefits for Museveni in the 1990s, when his government's willingness to undertake economic reform and to speak about the need to tackle HIV/AIDS made him a favorite of development officials in the UK and US.

Over time, this reputation became harder to sustain, both because economic growth started to slow and because Museveni's refusal to allow free and fair elections, or to respect constitutional term and age limits, called into question whether his regime was really committed to good governance. Despite this, Museveni's National Resistance Movement government has consistently referenced stability and the provision of development as the core touchstone of its message during election campaigns and moments of national celebration, a tendency that is beautifully encapsulated by the poem reproduced in Box 5.1.

### Box 5.1 "Revolutionary Presidents"

*The military victory of president Yoweri Museveni's National Resistance Movement over its opponents in January 1986 is celebrated annually in Uganda on the 27 January as "Liberation Day."*

*The day's festivities involve speeches and presentations of medals by Museveni as well as a range of readings and poems aimed at praising and thanking the ruling party for its role in developing Uganda's economy and bringing peace to the country as part of the regime's developmental approach to governance. There follows a poem recited to Museveni by a local primary school during the 2018 celebrations—held in Arua, northern Uganda. As you can see, the focus is placed squarely on celebrating the president as a revolutionary reformer himself, rather than his party or government, and characterizing him as almost singly responsible for returning peace and prosperity to Uganda after years of dictatorship and misrule during the 1970s and 1980s.*

#### Revolutionary Presidents

Revolutionary presidents, revolutionary presidents, revolutionary presidents;[3]
Revolutionary presidents are rare, scarce, golden, in a few lucky countries.

---

[3] The recitation of the poem (and full Liberation Day 2018 ceremony) can be viewed at https://www.youtube.com/watch?v=s_rcSYL7hxw. The poem begins at 4:27:40.

In certain heroic changes for national unity; development is what they are remembered for.

His Excellency Yoweri Kaguta Museveni: the only revolutionary president since 1986 to date;

*(Audience applauds)*

You have rehabilitated the fractured Uganda by war, during harsh regimes of untested leaders:

Maintaining national stability!

No more rebellions!

No more tribalism and racism!

No more Trypanosomiasis [also known as sleeping sickness]

We are a stable country.

Giving birth to East African Community is your brainchild.

Oh great president! Your revolutionary dress will never fit grumbling political opponents;

*(Audience cheers and applauds)*

Revolutionary president, revolutionary president, revolutionary president;

Your range of vision passes through mountains, valleys, and the space,

Leading the country to her greatest political, social, and economic transformation.

Diversification of the economy!

Manufacturing and tourism industry!

Oil and gas exploration!

Operation wealth creation!

Local and foreign investors in business and job creation!

Providing safe water and better healthcare services!

Boreholes all over!

Rural urban piped water supply!

Number one for immunization!

Reduced mortality rate!

Basic education through UPE [Universal Primary Education] and USE [Universal Secondary Education]!

Special needs education for handicaps!

Inclusive education for all!

Girl Child education is number-one priority.

More children enrolled in schools! Improve infrastructural development and telecommunications!

Major roads tarmacked and with electricity in all towns!

*(silence and inaudible conversation among the poem reciters)*

Revolutionary president! Revolutionary president! Revolutionary president! What a messiah!

But let Yoweri Kaguta to save Uganda from any political, social, or economic crisis.

The old know all about the gun;

Everlasting peace is their expectation.

The young, energetic have just heard and seen the gun: following political liars is their excitement;

The children of liberation government only know about food, classroom, and sleeping;

Stable government gives them hope of life.

Oh baba! Father of the nation!

Have a system, the children starve, for old age is never inability.

For God and to my country!

*The 2018 Liberation Day was held against the backdrop of Ugandan legislators' efforts to further lengthen Museveni's time in office by removing the constitutional provision that only those below the age of seventy-five can stand for president (Museveni was seventy-three at the time of the celebrations). This explains the final part of the poem ("old age is never inability") and the comments which immediately followed from the event's master of ceremonies, President's Office Minister Esther Mbayo:*

Your Excellency, I request that you have a photo posed with these children and with that they have said it all: as a revolutionary president, Uganda still needs you, Your Excellency.

It is this combination of holding elections and delivering on the economy that marks out authoritarianism 2.0 in the African context. Whereas the authoritarian states of the 1970s and 1980s banned opposition parties, contemporary authoritarian governments have found new ways to maintain political control by reintroducing multiparty elections and then manipulating them. Along with the provision of stability and development, this has enabled a number of governments to cultivate domestic support and international respectability despite the fact that their power ultimately rests on similar foundations to the authoritarian states of the past.

# IS AUTHORITARIANISM "BETTER" THAN DEMOCRACY?

This chapter has provided evidence that some authoritarian states have performed better than their democratic counterparts when it comes to promoting economic development. In turn, this has led to an important debate about whether democracy or authoritarian systems are more effective in the African context. There are usually three related components to this conversation. The first focuses on whether or not multiparty elections are "un-African"—in other words, whether they represent an external Western value system that is unsuitable. Those who make this argument typically suggest that African traditions contain elements of democracy but that these became manifest in a different way in the form of consensus politics. For example, George Ayittey (2006), a Ghanaian economist, has argued that multiparty politics "is possible but not suitable for Africa." Instead, he argues that Africa should pursue a form of consensus government that would be more reflective of traditional practices.

It is important to note that Ayittey is not arguing for authoritarian government—instead, he is proposing that African states "turn back the clock" and follow what he sees as a more culturally appropriate method for resolving disputes and agreeing government policy. This, he argues, would be equally democratic, but more effective. If African countries were to follow this pathway, they would move away from competitive politics to focus more on the role of traditional leaders (chiefs), who would consult their citizens through meetings and discussions, seeking to reach a position that everyone is happy with; a position not dissimilar to that of Nyerere, described in Chapter 2.

The second component of this conversation focuses on whether authoritarian states have advantages when it comes to development. The success of Ethiopia and Rwanda, and the rise of China to the status of global economic superpower, have demonstrated that democracies do not always outperform other types of political system when it comes to development. Indeed, there are some good reasons for thinking that authoritarian states may have an edge when it comes to forcing through painful but necessary economic reforms. Most obviously, authoritarian leaders face fewer constraints when it comes to making the kind of tough decisions that will be unpopular in the short run but are necessary for long-term success. By contrast, democratic governments must always think about the next election, which can lead to a problematic focus on keeping voters happy in the short term. This is one reason, for example, that so many democracies have struggled to deal with issues such as pensions crises and global warming, where the benefit of solving the problem will only be realized in many years' time, but the cost of doing so will be felt today.

A third less common but nonetheless important strand to this debate is that in some cases authoritarian regimes have achieved great progress on issues that are highly valued by democrats, such as disabled rights and gender equality. For example, despite not allowing opposition parties to compete freely in elections, President Yoweri Museveni's Uganda has some of the most progressive legislation on the rights of people with disabilities in the entire African continent—including reserved seats at each level of government. Moreover, while it might initially seem surprising that authoritarian governments would outperform their democratic counterparts on issues such as equality, this has clearly occurred in a number of cases with regards to gender equality in parliament, as we discuss at greater length in Box 5.2.

---

**Box 5.2   The Challenge of Promoting Gender Equality**

In the vast majority of countries around the world, women are underrepresented in parliament. While most societies have slightly more men than women, most legislatures are male dominated.

It is tempting to think that democracies should be good at promoting gender equality because they are supposed to be more inclusive and to protect the rights and interests of all citizens—but this is not actually the case. Many of the oldest democracies in the world actually perform particularly badly when it comes to the proportion of women in parliament. According to data collected by the Inter-Parliamentary Union, in 2016 women made up just 30 percent of the House of Commons in the United Kingdom and 20 percent in the US House of Representatives—a figure that puts the United States behind both Equatorial Guinea and Saudi Arabia.

Some of Africa's authoritarian states look much better by comparison. Partly because they have introduced gender quotas to guarantee that the proportion of men elected cannot exceed a certain threshold—often around 60 percent—women represent 36 percent of the legislature in Burundi and 34 percent in Uganda. The situation in Rwanda is even more impressive, because 61 percent of the seats in the Chamber of Deputies are held by women—the highest proportion in the world. Outside of Africa, a number of other authoritarian states also perform well on this measure: the country with the second highest percentage of women in the legislature is Cuba, at 53 percent.

Of course, simply having more women in parliament does not mean that women's rights—such as the right to inherit land and to live free from gender-based violence—will be advanced. In an authoritarian context, women may not be able to translate their position in parliament into more progressive legislation, especially if one reason they were promoted was to make undemocratic political systems seem more acceptable. For example, some critics have accused Paul Kagame of "window dressing": increasing the number of women in his government so that he can use this as a way to create the false impression that his regime is inclusive.

It is also important not to assume that women will always want to speak to women's issues. Amina Mama (1995: 41) argues that when high-profile women—such as the First Lady (the wife of the president)—take over the leadership of women's movements, the result is often not feminism, which she sees as the liberation of women from oppression, but femocracy: "an anti-democratic female power structure which claims to exist for the advancement of ordinary women, but is unable to do so because it is dominated by a small clique of women whose authority derives from their being married to powerful men, rather than from any actions or ideas of their own."

However, while these are important caveats to keep in mind, a number of researchers have found that women in authoritarian legislatures in Africa are not just there for show. For example, Gretchen Bauer and Jennie Burnet (2013) conclude that female Rwandan legislators are broadly effective at representing women's interests at the national level and help to promote pro-women policies. Vibeke Wang (2013) comes to a similar conclusion regarding women parliamentarians in Uganda, where voters in each district elect a "Women's Representative" to parliament in addition to their constituency member of parliament.

This does not mean that authoritarian states always do better when it comes to promoting gender equality. Many undemocratic countries perform very badly and some democracies, such as Namibia and South Africa, do very well. But what it does mean is that there is no simple relationship between how democratic a country is and how it treats women—and this is the kind of unsettling reality that those seeking to justify authoritarian regimes often seize upon to make their case.

The combination of these three arguments has made some African leaders and citizens question whether democracy should actually be the goal for their countries, or to suggest that the concept needs to be "Africanized" before it can be successfully deployed on the continent. Indeed, it is just this kind of argument that Rwandan president Paul Kagame made in a 2017 interview with the *Financial Times* newspaper, which is reproduced in Box 5.3.

### Box 5.3   Time for "African Democracy"?

The following text comes from an interview between the British newspaper *The Financial Times* and the Rwandan President Paul Kagame that was published on August 27, 2017. The full transcript is available at https://www.ft.com/content/0ec9dc4e-8976-11e7-8bb1-5ba57d47eff7

*Financial Times*: "Westerners would tend to see this as an authoritarian society. But you may well see what you have created as a different type of democracy, one based perhaps on traditions that maybe go back hundreds of years, and one that maybe has its roots in the RPF, the camps of Uganda, the fact that this is how you came to power?"

*Paul Kagame*: "Maybe let's talk about democracy, and not western democracy, because is there something called democracy without putting the western thing? If we can do that, maybe that's where I stand. And I look at the ingredients of democracy generally, not making it western, because making it western raises many other questions.

"I'm not British, I'm not American, I'm not French, Whatever thing they practice, that is their business. I am an African, I'm Rwandese, and there must be universal principles and values that people want to identify with. I'm not here to champion western anything. There are things I like about the West, absolutely, and learn from and want to emulate. But this whole thing of measuring, you forget my conditions here in Rwanda or in Africa that affect me daily in my life, and you are telling me I should be like somebody else. My starting point is to tell you, please put that aside.

"Nothing is perfect, but I find [here] the principles and ingredients of a democratic society that answers to its people, that allows its people to make choices they want to make, to try and bring people together even with different outlooks, backgrounds, thinking, and work for the common goal. That is development of this Rwanda, this country. Western democracy answers to certain societies who are coming from a certain place. There are elements, good elements of democracy in what we are doing, but [it] doesn't immediately fit into the western democracy.

"For me to fit into western democracy, western democracy must be fitting into our lives that we have to live as a society maybe with different context and circumstances. So it is a debate that will go on for a long time, but at the same time my viewpoint, at least, is while the debate goes on we must be able to live our lives. We live a life, a real life. It's not utopian. And I have never come to terms with the idea that somebody else has the right to decide how I live my life, and I don't think that is part of democracy. Actually, if people believe in values and principles of democracy, I think wanting to dictate the choices and how people live their lives, other people, I think that falls short."

However, there are two reasons to be skeptical of this argument—especially when it is used to justify authoritarian forms of government. The first is that while Ayittey is right that there are many different ways to build a democracy, the politics of consensus has often been used to legitimate repression and the abuse of power. As we have seen, the one-party states of the 1970s and 1980s were often justified on the basis that unity was needed for development and that one-party rule was more "African" than multiparty rule, but in reality they were often exclusive and failed to protect the interests of minority communities. Moreover, while the notion of traditional leaders consulting with their communities may be appealing in some ways, the fact that most chiefs are men means that "traditional" mechanisms would need to be significantly reformed if they were not to exclude women from political leadership. There are also serious questions about whether it would be possible to use such an approach to make national-level policy in countries with multiple ethnic groups and tens of millions of citizens.

The second problem with this argument is that the evidence suggests that Ethiopia, Rwanda, and Uganda are the exception rather than the norm. Foa's research, referred to above, reveals that the recent "authoritarian revival" that has led to improved state capacity in terms of the rule of law and the development of national infrastructure has been driven by China and a number of other countries such as Vietnam. The picture is very different in sub-Saharan Africa, where, instead of closing the gap on democratic states, authoritarian states have on average either stagnated or fallen even further behind.

Similarly, although a small number of authoritarian states perform well when it comes to gender equality, as we discussed in Box 4.2, these countries are not representative. Some of the least gender-balanced parliaments in the world can be found in African authoritarian states—including those of Central African Republic (9 percent female), Democratic Republic of Congo (9 percent), Djibouti (11 percent), and Swaziland (6 percent)—while perhaps the most authoritarian regime on the continent, that of Eritrea, has long struggled to return enough women to power even to meet declared gender quotas in local elections (Rigat 2016).[4]

Other features of some of the authoritarian parliaments that do well on gender balance also demonstrate that they are much less impressive when it comes to other forms of equality. Ugandan parliamentarians, for example, gained international notoriety during the 2010s for supporting legislation targeting one of the most vulnerable groups in many African states: sexual minorities. Referred to in the Ugandan media as the "Kill the Gays Bill," the Anti-Homosexuality Act signed into law by President Yoweri Museveni in February 2014 expanded the range of penalties to be meted out to those accused of "the offence of homosexuality" (illegal in Uganda since the colonial era). It also created a new offence of "aggravated homosexuality" and criminalized the act of "aiding, abetting, counselling or procuring another to engage in an act of homosexuality"—incentivizing employers to dismiss homosexual employees and landlords to evict homosexual tenants (Nyanzi and Karamagi 2015).

---

[4] At the time of writing, Eritrea has never held national-level elections.

This raises an important question: what explains why so many African states are stagnating and have not participated in the "authoritarian revival" identified by Foa? One answer is that key political institutions are often particularly weak, both in terms of their infrastructural capacity and their political independence, as a result of the colonial legacy discussed in Chapter 1 and, in many countries, long-running civil conflicts that have militated against state building. Another is that the emergence of big men and neo-patrimonial politics has enabled leaders to undermine institutional checks and balances and so entrench themselves in power in some—but by no means all—African states. In turn, this has facilitated higher levels of corruption—a problem that is exacerbated when governments are undemocratic and so face even fewer constraints. As a result, when authoritarian governments in Africa have tried to take a dominant role in plotting a new political and economic course for their countries, it has often resulted in greater waste and inefficiency, harming economic growth.

Rwanda has not fallen in to this trap because its leader has been able to exert tight top-down control and has insisted on keeping corruption to a minimum. This has meant that income generated by the ruling party's control of the economy is reinvested rather than simply fueling corruption—a model that David Booth and Frederick Golooba-Mutebi (2012) have called "developmental patrimonialism" in recognition of its capacity to create jobs and build a national infrastructure. But the kind of rigid top-down control that such a system requires is not present in most countries – which feature more ethnic groups, more big men, and greater political competition – and so the same policies have very different consequences. As a result, while a small number of authoritarian states have performed very well, on average they are outperformed by democracies. According to research by Takaaki Masaki and Nicolas Van de Walle (2014), when the entire continent is taken into account, it becomes clear that democracies have achieved higher economic growth than authoritarian states—and the longer a country is democratic, the greater the benefit.

## CONCLUSION: THE POWER OF LABELS

Researchers who work on politics often use labels as a shortcut to describe a particular country. Saying that Rwanda is authoritarian, or that Botswana is a democracy, is a lot quicker and easier than specifying exactly how free and open politics is in these countries. But while they are useful, such labels also simplify reality. We therefore need to make sure that when we use them we do not lose sight of the fact that terms like "authoritarian" may obscure as much as they reveal.

This chapter has demonstrated that while authoritarian and democratic states differ in the way that the government comes to power, this does not necessarily tell us how good these states are at providing development, fighting corruption, and pursuing gender equality. It is not the case that democracies are always better at representing the needs of poor and marginalized groups simply because the government is fairly elected. Similarly, it is not the case that authoritarian governments are always less inclusive because they hold power through a combination of coercion and co-optation. Instead, it is important to keep in mind that there is great variation within the category of authoritarian states and within the category of democratic countries. In the previous section, we argued that on the whole democracies tend to perform better than authoritarian states in Africa on the issues that really matter. But we also noted that there were exceptions to this rule.

It is also important to think carefully about labels because they have the power to legitimate governments and political systems. Throughout postcolonial African history, political leaders have sought to look democratic in order to appear respectable, minimize criticism, and access international financial assistance. As we saw in the last chapter, some authoritarian states have been able to secure Western funding despite performing poorly on a range of criteria—for example, because they were important allies on foreign policy issues—but it remains true that for many countries that lack international leverage, appearing to be democratic can unlock greater financial benefits. Faking democracy is also a popular strategy because few leaders like to think of themselves as being authoritarian bullies—even notorious autocrats such as Idi Amin or Robert Mugabe were desperate to be seen as popular leaders beloved by their own people.

This set of motivations helps to explain why so many authoritarian political parties include the word "democratic" in their name. For example, Paul Biya's party in Cameroon is called the Cameroon People's Democratic Movement. Similarly, Omar Bongo's political vehicle in Gabon, which he ruled with an iron first for forty-two years, was called the Gabonese Democratic Party. The challenge for those studying African politics is to work out which parties and countries deserve such a label and which are claiming it illegitimately.

# REFERENCES

Ayittey, George. *Indigenous African Institutions*. Leiden: Brill, 2006.

Bauer, Gretchen, and Burnet, Jennie E. "Gender Quotas, Democracy, and Women's Representation in Africa: Some Insights from Democratic Botswana and Autocratic Rwanda." *Women's Studies International Forum* 41, no. 2 (2013): 103–12.

Brown, Stephen. "Authoritarian Leaders and Multiparty Elections in Africa: How Foreign Donors Help to Keep Kenya's Daniel arap Moi in Power." *Third World Quarterly* 22, no. 5 (2001): 725–739.

Booth, David, and Frederick Golooba-Mutebi. "Developmental Patrimonialism? The Case of Rwanda." *African Affairs* 111, no. 444 (2012): 379–403.

Cheeseman, Nic. "African elections as vehicles for change." *Journal of Democracy* 21, no. 4 (2010): 139–153.

Cheeseman, Nic. *Democracy in Africa: Successes, Failures, and the Struggle for Political Reform*. Cambridge, Cambridge University Press, 2015.

Cheeseman, Nic, and Brian Klaas. *How to Rig an Election*. New Haven, CT: Yale University Press, 2018.

Des Forges, Alison Liebhafsky, Human Rights Watch, and International Federation of Human Rights. *"Leave None to Tell the Story": Genocide in Rwanda*. Vol. 3169, no. 189. New York: Human Rights Watch, 1999.

Foa, Roberto. "The Challenge of Authoritarian Modernization." Research Paper, Canberra, Australia, April 17, 2018.

Mama, Amina. "Feminism or Femocracy? State Feminism and Democratization in Nigeria." *African Development* 22, no. 3–4 (1995): 37–58.

Masaki, Takaaki, and Nicolas Van de Walle. *The Impact of Democracy on Economic Growth in Sub-Saharan Africa, 1982–2012*. No. 2014/057. WIDER Working Paper, 2014.

Nyanzi, Stella, and Andrew Karamagi. "The Social-Political Dynamics of the Anti-Homosexuality Legislation in Uganda." *Agenda* 29, no. 1 (2015): 24–38.

Rigat, Tesgamichael. "Women's Participation after Independence." Paper presented at International Conference on Eritrean Studies, Asmara, Eritrea, June 22, 2016.

Schedler, Andreas. "The Menu of Manipulation." *Journal of Democracy* 13, no. 2 (2002): 36–50.

Throup, David, and Charles Hornsby. *Multi-party Politics in Kenya: The Kenyatta & Moi States & the Triumph of the System in the 1992 Election*. Athens: Ohio University Press, 1998.

Wang, Viveke. "Women Changing Policy Outcomes: Learning from Pro-Women Legislation in the Ugandan Parliament." *Women's Studies International Forum* 41, no. 2 (2013): 113–21.

## SUGGESTED READINGS

Ajulu, Rok. "Politicised Ethnicity, Competitive Politics and Conflict in Kenya: A Historical Perspective." *African Studies* 61, no. 2 (2002): 51–68.

Ake, Claude. *Democracy and Development in Africa.* Washington, DC: Brookings Institution Press, 2001.

Levitsky, Steven, and Lucan A. Way. *Competitive Authoritarianism: Hybrid Regimes after the Cold War.* Cambridge: Cambridge University Press, 2010.

Matfess, Hilary. "Rwanda and Ethiopia: Developmental Authoritarianism and the New Politics of African Strong Men." *African Studies Review* 58, no. 2 (2015): 181–204.

Museveni, Yoweri. *What Is Africa's Problem?* Minneapolis: University of Minnesota Press, 2000.

Ottaway, Marina. *Africa's New Leaders: Democracy or State Reconstruction?* Washington, DC: Brookings Institution Press, 1999.

Prempeh, H. Kwasi. "Progress and Retreat in Africa: Presidents Untamed." *Journal of Democracy* 19, no. 2 (2008): 109–23.

Tripp, Aili Mari. *Museveni's Uganda: Paradoxes of Power in a Hybrid Regime.* Boulder, CO: Lynne Rienner, 2010.

# Conclusion

*Everyday Life, Resistance, and the Future of African Authoritarianism*

In October 2014, President Blaise Compaoré of Burkina Faso became the first African president to be directly forced from office by popular protests. Opposed to his attempt to amend the Burkinabé constitution and extend his rule, as many as one million protestors—galvanized by opposition parties—took to the streets across the country in what came to be called a popular uprising. Thousands stormed the parliament building (the *Assemblée Nationale*), toppled statues of Compaoré, and amassed around the presidential palace and army headquarters. After a vain effort to buy time, he resigned and fled to Côte d'Ivoire.

Compaoré had come to power in a coup d'état nearly thirty years previously and had overseen the establishment of an increasingly authoritarian government. His overthrow was largely unexpected, especially within the international community, as was Yahya Jammeh's defeat in Gambia's 2016 presidential election, described in this book's introduction. Compaoré's downfall therefore underlines just how much of what goes on within authoritarian regimes is hidden to outside observers. The voluntary retirement of Angola's José Eduardo Dos Santos—one of the world's longest-ruling presidents—in September 2017 also took most by surprise, as did the Zimbabwean army's removal of president Robert Mugabe two months later. Even the majority of Zimbabwe scholars had assumed until days earlier that Mugabe—in power since 1980—would leave office only at a time of his, or nature's, choosing.

This is not to say that there are no ways for careful observers to work out which way the wind is blowing. In the case of Burkina Faso, it was known several years prior to Compaoré's removal that the idea of abolishing the constitutional two-term presidential limit was very unpopular. The Afrobarometer, a pan-African network that undertakes surveys of African populations on political, economic, and social matters, conducted a survey in the country between 2011 and 2013, which found that nearly two-thirds of those spoken to believed that "the constitution should limit the president to serving a maximum of two terms in office."[1] Few could have predicted, though, that this would come to a head in a revolution that would see the president deposed—an unprecedented event on the continent, and one characterized by some as Burkina Faso's "Arab Spring."

The pro-democracy disposition of the public in Burkina Faso is reflected across most of the continent, in both democratic and authoritarian states. However, while the vast majority of people across Africa support the idea of democracy, public attitudes on this issue are complex. Between 2002 and 2015, the Afrobarometer interviewed nationally representative samples of respondents in sixteen different countries in sub-Saharan Africa every few years. On average, the proportion of people who said that they prefer to live under a democratic government increased from 63 percent in 2002/3 to 75 percent in 2011/2013, while the proportion of people rejecting the idea of one-man rule (i.e., a personal dictatorship) increased from 76 percent to 84 percent over the same period. In other words, both support for democracy and rejection of authoritarian rule strengthened in these years.

However, the Afrobarometer also has a number of cautionary tales to tell. From 2011 onward, support for democracy began to decline, falling to 68 percent in 2014/2015. As Robert Mattes and Michael Bratton (2016) explain, this recent trend demonstrates that while most Africans want to live under a democratic government, such attitudes cannot be taken for granted. Moreover, their analysis reveals that one of the main factors that leads to falling support for democracy as a system of government is poor-quality elections. This is a major challenge to the

---

[1] Afrobarometer's survey questionnaires and results, together with extensive scholarly analyses and working papers, can be found at www.afrobarometer.org.

consolidation of democracy, given the capacity of authoritarian leaders to manipulate elections in order to remain in power, as we saw in the last chapter.

To conclude our discussion of authoritarianism in Africa, we consider how citizens and voters are resisting repression and responding to the possibility of democracy, before looking ahead to the future of politics on the continent. If the evidence provided in this book is anything to go by, we should not expect authoritarianism to simply fade away over time. There is nothing inevitable about the victory of democracy, and recent economic and international trends suggest that the continent's future is likely to see a continuation of the struggles of the past thirty years.

## PUBLIC ATTITUDES TOWARD DEMOCRACY AND AUTHORITARIANISM

While it is true that most Africans want to live under a democracy, it is also important to recognize that there are considerable variations both across countries and within countries. As you can see in Figure C.1, a majority of citizens believe that democracy is preferable to any other form of government in every country surveyed by the Afrobarometer except for Madagascar (just 47 percent) and Swaziland renamed Eswatini in 2018 (43 percent). It is therefore clear that whatever authoritarian leaders might say, there is very limited support for a return to the one-party states and military governments of the 1980s. But while overwhelming majorities support democracy in Uganda (81 percent) and Zambia (82 percent), we see more modest figures in Malawi (62 percent) and Namibia (65 percent).

There are also significant variations within each country. In general, although poorer, rural and less well educated citizens prefer democracy, those who have a university education, middle-class job, and live in urban areas are more likely to both support a broad range of democratic principles and reject authoritarian alternatives. This is unsurprising, as surveys often find that people who have greater access to information and education are more critical of the government, and more determined to place constraints on those in power. Given that African states are undergoing rapid processes of urbanization and that increasing numbers of young people are being educated and going to university, support for democracy is likely to strengthen in the future, other things being equal.

This trend raises the important and tricky question of what support for democracy really means. When someone says that she prefers

Support for democracy

| Country | Statement 3 | Statement 2 | Statement 1 | Don't know |
|---------|---------|---------|---------|---------|
| Benin | 13% | 13% | 72% | 1% |
| Burkina Faso | 18% | 17% | 63% | 2% |
| Botswana | 8% | 10% | 80% | 2% |
| Cape Verde | 15% | 10% | 70% | 4% |
| Côte d'Ivoire | 11% | 5% | 77% | 7% |
| Gabon | 16% | 11% | 72% | * |
| Ghana | 5% | 12% | 81% | 2% |
| Guinea | 12% | 11% | 76% | |
| Kenya | 10% | 12% | 67% | 12% |
| Lesotho | 24% | 18% | 52% | 6% |
| Madagascar | 28% | 14% | 47% | 11% |
| Malawi | 11% | 24% | 62% | 3% |
| Mali | 13% | 19% | 67% | * |
| Mauritius | 9% | 6% | 78% | 6% |
| Namibia | 20% | 13% | 65% | 3% |
| Niger | 16% | 12% | 69% | 3% |
| Nigeria | 15% | 15% | 69% | * |
| Senegal | 9% | 6% | 82% | 3% |
| Swaziland | 20% | 32% | 43% | 5% |
| Tanzania | 9% | 8% | 78% | 6% |
| Togo | 14% | 8% | 75% | 3% |
| Uganda | 8% | 5% | 81% | 7% |
| Zambia | 6% | 9% | 82% | 3% |
| Zimbabwe | 13% | 5% | 75% | 7% |

0%      100%

- Statement 3: Doesn't matter
- Statement 2: Sometimes non-democratic preferable
- Statement 1: Democracy preferable
- Don't know

**FIGURE C.1** Support for democracy in Africa, 2016–18.

to live under a democracy in a survey, how strong is this belief? And what kind of democracy is it that people have in mind? The evidence from a number of different Afrobarometer questions is that African societies have fairly standard democratic beliefs—that is, they believe that elections are the best way to select the government and that it is important to place some constraints on the president or prime minister. But the very same citizens are often also concerned that unconstrained political competition could spiral out of control and lead to conflict and instability. As a result, support for accountability is often balanced by support for consensus and unity.

Thus, while large majorities in most countries support the principle of presidential term limits, they also tend to place much more trust in the president than in opposition parties. Indeed, in 2015, the Afrobarometer revealed a 20-point gap between public approval of ruling parties and their opposition counterparts. The reason for this is that many citizens continue to connect opposition parties with heated competition, political instability, and the potential for violence.

Similarly, although 71 percent of those who respond to surveys want parties and leaders that lose an election to play a "watchdog" role, they do not want them to do so in a confrontational way. Instead, 60 percent say that election losers should "set aside their differences" and "concentrate on cooperating with government" (Logan 2015). This is an important reminder that while democracy may be a central priority for almost all African societies, stability and unity are not far behind. Development also remains a serious concern, in part because many African countries continue to feature high levels of unemployment and poverty. One of the reasons that so many people threw their weight behind democratization in the 1980s was the belief that it would lead to both political freedoms *and* economic recovery. This means that support for democracy may be undermined if a "strong leader" is seen to be essential to both national harmony and development.

As we have seen, belief in the importance of unity and stability is rooted in past experience and what we might call "political education"—the efforts of successive leaders to legitimate their rule through a combination of argumentation, propaganda, and education. Citizens who lived under one-party states were socialized for many years into a political worldview that reified consensus over competition. In Tanzania, for example, the ruling party did not just play on popular concerns about the potential for conflict; it also actively attempted to re-educate Tanzanians to suppress individual desires in favor of the national interest. Tanzanian President Julius Nyerere, for example, often spoke about the value of community and the need to work for "the common good," suggesting that these Tanzanian and African ideals stood in contrast to those promoted by the colonial power (see Box C.1). This strong focus on unity, and on consensus building, as a form of "African democracy" proved to be highly effective in muting support for greater individual freedoms and political liberalization. Even today, Tanzania remains one of the countries surveyed by the Afrobarometer in which people are least likely to support multiparty politics and to reject the principle of one-party rule.

## Box C.1   Education for Self-Reliance

*This text is an excerpt from one of President Julius Nyerere's writings on education, which was issued in 1967 in a volume entitled* Freedom and Socialism.

Our people in the rural areas, as well as their government, must organize themselves co-operatively and work for themselves through working for the community of which they are members. Our village life, as well as our state organization, must be based on the principle of socialism and that equality in work and return which is part of it.

This is what our educational system has to encourage. It has to foster the social goals of living together, and working together, for the common good. It has to prepare our young people to play a dynamic and constructive part in the development of a society in which all members share fairly in the good or bad fortune of the group, and in which progress is measured in terms of human well-being, not prestige buildings, cars, or other such things, whether privately or publicly owned. Our education must therefore inculcate a sense of commitment to the total community, and help the pupils to accept the values appropriate to our kind of future, not those appropriate to our colonial past.

This means that the educational system of Tanzania must emphasize cooperative endeavour, not individual advancement; it must stress concepts of equality and the responsibility to give service which goes with any special ability, whether it be in carpentry, in animal husbandry, or in academic pursuits. And, in particular, our education must counteract the temptation to intellectual arrogance; for this leads to the well-educated despising those whose abilities are non-academic or who have no special abilities but are just human beings. Such arrogance has no place in a society of equal citizens.

One consequence of historical experiences like that of Tanzania is that citizens in many African countries are supportive of a kind of consensual democracy, in which the right of citizens to elect their leaders and hold them to account is balanced against a respect for authority and a strong desire to avoid major political disagreements. In turn, this generates significant problems for opposition parties, which know that they need to push for democratic reforms to increase their chance of winning elections, but may be punished by voters if they are seen to be a destabilizing force. It also means that authoritarian leaders can increase popular support for their rule if they are able to persuade their people that conflict and poverty are inevitable unless tight political control is exerted from the top down.

These historical legacies and contemporary attitudes demonstrate that authoritarian rule is not simply a way station on the inevitable journey to democracy. Instead, it should be understood in its own right and taken seriously as a phenomenon that has meaning and, critically, may also have legitimacy for some populations and communities. Indeed, as we saw in Chapter 5, it has become easier for leaders to legitimate authoritarian rule in recent years as a result of nondemocratic "success stories" both in Africa and around the world. The high levels of economic growth in Ethiopia, Rwanda, and China, combined with the great controversy surrounding multiparty elections in many countries, has made it possible to argue that promoting democracy might not be the best way to secure development and stability after all.

## EVERYDAY AUTHORITARIANISM

Understanding the future of authoritarianism is complicated by the fact that we often lack good quality information about critical issues such as the state of the economy and popular attitudes in the most repressive states. For example, although surveys can provide fascinating insights into how citizens think, and have proved to be reliable even in a number of authoritarian states, conducting them in the most repressive countries poses profound challenges—not only in terms of accessing a representative sample of society but also securing candid answers from respondents, who may be worried about state authorities finding out if they have criticized the political system. This book has underlined the importance of understanding the historical development and context of African authoritarianism in order to comprehend political dynamics in the present. What we want to emphasize in this final chapter, though, is how little we know about some aspects of authoritarianism, both historically and in the contemporary era.

This does not mean that we cannot know anything about how communities and peoples in authoritarian Africa experience and perceive their governments. What it does mean, though, is that we sometimes need to make the effort to look beyond traditional sources of data on public opinion—notably opinion polls and the press. Indeed, in some authoritarian states the only media reporting that is accessible is that disseminated by the government itself. Such sources tell us little about everyday experiences; all we can really learn is what the authoritarian state wishes domestic and international audiences to know, and to believe. This has been the case, for example, in post-2001 Eritrea, where the only domestic television and radio channels have been broadcast from the Ministry of Information and via the state-owned ERiTV. ERiTV's slogan is "serving the truth," though it is, in essence, a propaganda mouthpiece combining pro-government messaging with programs celebrating a particular vision of Eritrean history.

If opinion poll data are unavailable and the media are biased, where can we look to gain insights into authoritarian states? One answer is the world of art and culture, which has provided an important space for critical views of authoritarian states to be expressed. It has also afforded an opportunity for African peoples and communities to articulate their personal fears and political grievances beyond the heavily regulated realm of formal politics and to have their voices heard. In 2005, for example, the Zimbabwean police and military demolished thousands of informal settlements in the country in an operation called *Murambatsvina* ("clear out the rubbish"). Officially, this strategy was designed to crack down on illegal housing and criminal activities and to prevent the spread of infectious diseases. But in reality it had a strong political motivation. Urban voters had heavily backed Robert Mugabe's main rival, Morgan Tsvangirai, in presidential elections in 2002, and in Senate and House of Assembly elections in 2005. By destroying the areas in which many of these people lived in such a violent way, Mugabe demonstrated the high cost of standing up to his regime.

But as with any large-scale act of political violence, many of those who suffered were not politically active. Among the estimated 700,000 people who lost their homes and livelihoods in a matter of weeks were a group of women in Killarney, a suburb of Bulawayo, Zimbabwe's second city. *Murambatsvina* was a deeply frightening and confusing experience for these women, who lost relatives (including a baby) in the violence and did not understand why the government was targeting them in this way.

Several years later, the women of Killarney worked together to create an *arpillera* (a patchwork) to express the fear and chaos they had experienced. The *arpillera*, displayed by the women themselves (see Image C.1), was called "The day we will never forget" and depicts soldiers and policemen with dogs beating civilians and burning down their houses and churches. The power of the *arpillera* comes partly

**IMAGE C.1**  Resistance and memory in Zimbabwe. "The day we will never forget" (2012). Collective work by Killarney girls, facilitated by Shari Eppel, Solidarity Peace Trust of Zimbabwe. Photo: Shari Eppel. © Conflict Textiles.[2]

from its juxtaposition of bright colors and disturbing images and partly from its deeply personal character. The piece was a joint effort which the community developed together, incorporating parts of their clothing, furniture, and even hair into the imagery. The aim was to enunciate an experience which was difficult—and politically sensitive—to represent in words and to show the world the violence the community had suffered at the hands of their own government. Since its creation, the *arpillera* has been displayed in exhibitions across the world—from Buenos Aires to Birmingham and from Cape Town to Geneva.

Humor has also been an important means of expression in African authoritarian states, and this continues today, with serious messages and critiques embedded within ostensibly blithe cartoons or performances. In the dying years of Daniel arap Moi's dictatorship in Kenya,

---

[2] For more information, see http://cain.ulster.ac.uk/conflicttextiles/search-quilts/fulltextiles/?id=263 (accessed September 6, 2019).

for example, artist Godfrey "Gado" Mwampembwa became famous for his scathing depictions of political corruption and hypocrisy in the well-read *Daily Nation* newspaper. By using beautifully drawn cartoons to lampoon those in power, Gado is able to communicate an idea much more directly and effectively than most journalists or researchers—especially for those who have limited literacy. He is also able to use humor and symbolism to get away with implying things that, if they were written down, might lead to a reporter being arrested.

One of his most celebrated cartoons draws on the notion of the electoral college in the United States – the body that elects the US President – to characterize the Kenyan general election of 2017 (see Image C.2). In the top half of the image, Gado depicts the main opposition leader, Raila Odinga, backed by what he calls the "popular vote"—the ordinary people. By contrast, in the bottom half of the image, he shows the incumbent president, Uhuru Kenyatta, backed not by the voters but by an "electoral college." However, while the electoral college in the United States is made up of elected and appointed representatives of the country's states, Gado depicts the Kenyan president as being backed by the leaders of the country's security forces.

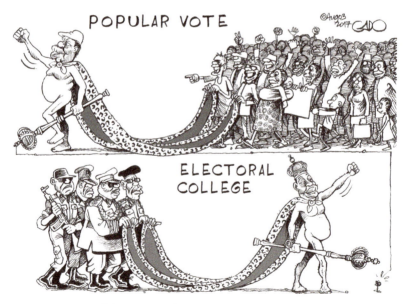

**IMAGE C.2**    Gado's cartoon of the 2017 Kenyan presidential election.
*Source*: www.gadocartoons.com

His point is clear: winning the popular vote may not win you the election unless you also have the support of this unrepresentative "electoral college." Real power lies not with the people, but with those who control violence.

This reflects a long tradition of speaking truth to power within African politics. During the one-party states of the 1980s, it was typically too dangerous for newspapers to criticize the president explicitly, but those who wished to speak truth to power had two other options. First, they could outline the failings of a specific policy, being careful to make it clear that a minister or advisor had led the president astray and that the president was therefore not to blame. Second, they could use satire to get their point across and evade punishment (Lungu 1986).

Satire is the use of exaggerated humor to expose how ridiculous a situation or a person really is. In many cases this involves explicitly naming the person—as in Gado's cartoons. But another form of satire is to highlight injustice or incompetence by telling stories with made-up characters with made-up names, which can provide another layer of protection against arrest in more authoritarian states. Because the characters are imaginary and no real names are used, satirists can claim to not be directly critiquing those in power—while in practice everybody knows who or what the story is referring to. In other words, satire can be like a kind of funny code, through which the writer can poke fun at those in power without using their names.

From the 1990s onward, the dawn of the Internet and social media has opened up new opportunities for artists and comedians to mock and condemn authoritarian African leaders. Images lampooning Sudan's authoritarian president, Omar al-Bashir, were shared across Sudan via Khalid Albaih's *Khartoon!* Facebook page (a *portmanteau* of "cartoon" and "Khartoum," Sudan's capital) from the late 2000s until his downfall in 2019. A popular online satirical television show—*Bisha TV*—has also been broadcast from the Nuba Mountains, the site of a long-running government counterinsurgency campaign, since the mid-2010s. Developed by a local artist, Ganja, *Bisha TV* focused on al-Bashir, who appeared as a puppet operated by Ganja, and his nefarious efforts to raise funds to wage war on his own people (Gilpin 2017; Gogineni 2017). To date, the series has been viewed by over one million people—including many in Sudan itself.

Humor has also been a vital coping mechanism for many of those living in authoritarian African states. In her study of "everyday authoritarianism" in early 2000s Eritrea, for example, Jennifer Riggan explains how a form of gallows humor developed among ordinary people in the country during this period (Riggan 2016). This particular coping mechanism became particularly associated with attempts to avoid—or warn of the proximity of—patrolling state operatives intent on forced recruitment of Eritreans into the country's open-ended national service program. Riggan's observation reveals something that is often overlooked in studies of authoritarian rule. While authoritarian systems can be brutal and violent—as the women of Killarney discovered in 2005—they are also, for many, the backdrop to everyday life. For outside observers, it is sometimes difficult to imagine that ordinary people live ordinary lives in authoritarian states such as Eritrea, and face the state's dictatorial excesses with a knowing joke as well as with fear and dread.

Humour, however, has its limits. In 2016, despite being one of the most famous and respected cartoonists on the continent, Gado's contract was not renewed by the *Daily Nation* newspaper. In interviews about this development, he has said that he was sure that this decision was motivated by government pressure to clamp down on dissident voices. Those brave enough to challenge the abuse of power in Eritrea often suffer even more severe punishments. Dawit Isaac, the cofounder of the newspaper *Setit*, was detained without trial in 2001 as part of a government crackdown on the press. Over fifteen years on, he remains behind bars, and his family does not even know where he is being held.

## THE REMARKABLE DURABILITY OF AFRICAN AUTHORITARIANISM

In the previous chapter we documented the capacity of authoritarian leaders to retain political control even after the introduction of multiparty elections in the 1990s. A similar story could also be told of the 2010s. Consider the case of Zimbabwe. When President Robert Mugabe was detained by the military in November 2017 in a bid to force him from power, hundreds of thousands of Zimbabweans marched in favor of a change of leader. Having been lauded as a visionary leader in the 1980s, Mugabe's rule had become characterized by economic failure, the collapse of key state institutions, and growing authoritarianism from the late 1990s onward. This included policies that were deliberately designed to harm communities who supported the opposition Movement for Democratic Change (MDC), such as the demolition of informal settlements in operations such as the one described earlier.

When Mugabe finally left power and was replaced by Emmerson Mnangagwa, many media commentators were hopeful that the country had at last turned the corner. Mnangagwa encouraged this sense of national renewal, pledging to revive the economy while promising to respect human rights and civil liberties. He also committed his government to holding early elections and allowing them to be monitored by a range of international observers. But many Zimbabwean citizens and those who had been following the country's politics for a long time were skeptical of these claims. Mnangagwa had previously played a key role in Mugabe's government, helping to devise the strategies that kept him in power. Critics also predicted that the central role played by the military in Mnangagwa's rise to power would give them greater influence in civilian politics—an argument that was confirmed when Mnangagwa appointed the head of the army, Constantino Chiwenga, as his vice president.

The election campaign initially provided some evidence in favor of the more optimistic interpretation of the prospects for democratic change. Mnangagwa followed through on many of his promises, and opposition candidates were able to campaign far more freely than in previous years. As a result, some observation groups such as a delegation from the African Union gave Mnangagwa's victory—he was pronounced the winner with 50.8 percent of the vote—a clean bill of health. However, other international observers such as the mission from the European Union and a joint delegation from the National Democratic Institute and the National Republic Institute of the United States were more critical, finding that low-level intimidation by figures aligned with the ruling party had generated a sense of fear and apprehension among voters. They also pointed out that the government had benefitted from unbalanced media coverage and the misuse of state officials and equipment.[3]

Events in-between polling day on July 30, 2018, and the official announcement of the result on August 3, 2018, cast further doubt on democratic credentials of the new regime. Concerned that a delay in releasing the figures meant that the election was being rigged, MDC

---

[3] The final report of the EU Observation Mission to Zimbabwe on the 2018 elections can be downloaded here: https://eeas.europa.eu/election-observation-missions/eom-zimbabwe-2018/51896/eueom-zimbabwe-final-report-2018-harmonised-elections_en. The final report of the NDI/IRI join mission can be downloaded here: https://www.ndi.org/publications/final-report-2018-zimbabwe-harmonized-elections-relative-improvements-insufficient

supporters began to protest, encouraged by their candidate, Nelson Chamisa, who claimed to have won the election. The response by the government was brutal. On August 1, government troops fired on opposition demonstrators they claimed had been rioting in Harare, the capital city, killing three people. A day later police raided the headquarters of the MDC, took sixteen people away for questioning, and confiscated equipment and documents. In the weeks that followed, MDC activists were harassed and an arrest warrant was issued for prominent MDC leader Tendai Biti on the dubious grounds that his statements around the elections had incited violence. The attempt to detain Biti caused particular concern to human rights groups, because he had previously been tortured for his opposition to the government of Robert Mugabe.

Later in 2018, the government also responded in a heavy-handed manner to popular protests against an increase in the price of fuel, cutting off access to the Internet, beating opposition supporters, and arresting protest leaders. Evidence of widespread human rights violations led many Zimbabweans to conclude that the transfer of power from Mugabe to Mnangagwa had not really been a new dawn and instead was simply a "face lift" that had changed the image of the government but had done little to change its underlying structure or inclinations. The sense of disappointment that this generated was aptly summed up by the first line of an article on the elections in the *Economist* magazine: "So much for a fresh start."

The fact that authoritarian strategies such as these have proved so durable over the last seventy years is powerful evidence that there is nothing inevitable about the rise of democracy. Instead, the fate of authoritarianism will depend on whether ruling elites are really willing to reform, the role played by international partners, and the strength of civil society groups and opposition parties.

## AFRICAN SOLUTIONS TO AFRICAN PROBLEMS?

Between 2000 and 2014, a number of African states, including Cameroon, Rwanda, Senegal, and South Africa, began to generate significantly higher levels of government revenue from domestic taxation, reducing their dependence on international donors. In turn, greater economic independence from foreign aid has contributed to a growing assertiveness and a more pronounced resistance to following Western democratic and economic models. In Kenya, for example, the growing tax take of the Kenya Revenue Authority (KRA) has reinforced the willingness of government leaders to challenge the authority of global institutions such as the International Criminal Court.

This trend implies that the future development of African states will be increasingly shaped by those on the continent and not by outside pressures. It is therefore important to ask whether there is any evidence of a growing consensus in favor of, or against, democratic reform among African leaders and organizations such as the African Union.

There have been a number of attempts to galvanize a movement in favor of better and more effective government—often referred to as "good governance"—since the reintroduction of multiparty politics. Perhaps most notably, in the 1990s the widespread belief that African people and societies were entering a new era in which they would be able to resolve the challenges faced led a number of prominent leaders and commentators to proclaim the onset of an "African renaissance." The central element of this school of thought was that by focusing on "African solutions to African problems" the continent could undergo a process of economic, social, political, and cultural renewal.

The term "African Renaissance" was first popularized by Cheikh Anta Diop in the mid-1940s but came to the fore during the tenure of South Africa's second president, Thabo Mbeki. In Mbeki's vision, the African Renaissance was to be Africa's third great emancipatory moment, following on from the first, decolonization, and the second, democratization. In September 1998, a conference was held on the African Renaissance in Johannesburg and a year later, the African Renaissance Institute was established in Pretoria, South Africa, on October 11, 1999.

Mbeki also pushed for his vision to be taken on by the Organization of African Unity (OAU) and later the African Union (AU) (Box C.2). As a result, many of his ideas—along with those of other leaders such as the Nigerian President Olusegun Obasanjo—came to be represented in the New Partnership for Africa's Development (NEPAD). Officially adopted at the 37th session of the Assembly of Heads of State and Government of the OAU in 2001, NEPAD was an economic development program designed to improve the performance of African states in a number of areas, increasing their political management and economic and corporate governance. One of the most high-profile components of the program was the African Peer Review Mechanism (APRM), which was intended to be a self-monitoring scheme through which African states would evaluate their progress against agreed targets, which would then be "peer reviewed" by other states.

## Box C.2 The African Union

*The Organization of African Union (OAU) was established in 1963 to fight colonialism and defend the sovereignty and independence of African states. Following the replacement of the OAU with the AU in 2002, this mission changed to focus on the achievement of a united, strong and independent Africa through the promotion of economic and political integration and peace. The AU is comprised of a number of bodies, including the Pan African Parliament, which meets in Midrand, South Africa; the AU Commission (or Secretariat), which is based in Addis Ababa, Ethiopia; and the Assembly of the African Union, which meets once a year. In effect, it is the Assembly, which is composed of the heads of state of member countries, which acts as the governing body of the AU and makes decisions on the most significant issues.*

*The stated objectives of the African Union include to achieve greater unity and solidarity between African countries and the peoples of Africa; promote peace, security, and stability on the continent; promote democratic principles and institutions, popular participation, and good governance; establish the necessary conditions which enable the continent to play its rightful role in the global economy and in international negotiations; promote and protect human and peoples' rights in accordance with the African Charter on Human and Peoples' Rights and other relevant human rights instruments; and to promote sustainable development at the economic, social, and cultural levels as well as the integration of African economies. These points are embodied in the AU's anthem, Let Us All Unite and Celebrate Together.*

*Let Us All Unite and Celebrate Together*
Let us all unite and celebrate together
The victories won for our liberation
Let us dedicate ourselves to rise together
To defend our liberty and unity
    O Sons and Daughters of Africa
    Flesh of the Sun and Flesh of the Sky
    Let us make Africa the Tree of Life
Let us all unite and sing together
To uphold the bonds that frame our destiny
Let us dedicate ourselves to fight together
For lasting peace and justice on earth

O Sons and Daughters of Africa
Flesh of the Sun and Flesh of the Sky
Let us make Africa the Tree of Life
Let us all unite and toil together
To give the best we have to Africa
The cradle of mankind and fount of culture
Our pride and hope at break of dawn
O Sons and Daughters of Africa
Flesh of the Sun and Flesh of the Sky
Let us make Africa the Tree of Life

*You can listen to the anthem here:*
https://au.int/en/about/symbols

Because the APRM included a focus on democracy and political governance as well as economic issues, it raised hopes that the African Union was beginning a process of transformation, from being a "dictators' talking club" to becoming a force for political transformation. However, although the APRM made a positive start, with thirty-five AU member states signing up, it made little progress thereafter. By 2016 only twenty of these countries had completed self-assessments, and since 2012 the mechanism has been largely inactive. At the same time, the APRM's voluntary self-assessment framework was heavily criticized for allowing poorly performing governments to avoid criticism.

The disappointing outcome of the APRM has been mirrored in other areas, such as the role of the AU when it comes to democracy and elections. On the one hand, the Constitutive Act of the African Union prohibits any member state in which there has been an unconstitutional transfer of power from taking part in AU activities, and the organization has been praised for its rejection of military coups. Most notably, Mauritania was suspended from the African Union following a coup in 2005, and pressure was applied to the ruling party in Malawi to ensure that president Bingu wa Mutharika was replaced by vice president Joyce Banda—as per the constitution—and not by the ruling party's favored candidate, the president's brother, following Mutharika's untimely death in office in 2012.[4]

---

[4] Mutharika's brother - Peter - was, however, elected President of Malawi - defeating Joyce Banda - in 2014.

On the other hand, the growing norm that unconstitutional power grabs are illegitimate has not always been matched by an equivalent commitment to free and fair elections or deepening democracy. As we saw in the introduction, the AU adopted a strong stance against efforts by the President of Gambia, Yahya Jammeh, to cling to power after he had a lost an election in December 2016. More generally, however, AU election observers are often perceived to be a "soft touch" (Okumu 2009), and while some coups have been condemned, the AU has been largely silent on democratic backsliding in countries such as Cameroon and Zimbabwe. Instead, figures such as Cameroon's Paul Biya have played a prominent leadership role within the AU itself, calling into question its credibility to speak with authority on these issues.

This apparent double standard is rooted in self-interest and the balance of power within the AU. All presidents have an incentive to take a stand against unconstitutional transfers of government such as the use of force to overthrow the regime because doing so reduces one of the main threats to their own hold on power. By contrast, measures to force *existing* governments to allow freer and fairer elections would make it harder for incumbent leaders to outmaneuver opposition parties, and so would weaken their hold on power. Leaders such as Biya have therefore been careful to avoid supporting the adoption of such policies with regard to other countries, because doing so would establish a precedent that could later be applied to their own states. This reality, along with the fact that so few African states are full democracies and a considerable number remain highly authoritarian, makes it extremely difficult to generate the necessary critical mass to use the AU effectively as a vehicle through which to protect political rights and civil liberties.

Whether or not the AU will become a more effective force for democratization in the future will therefore depend, in large part, on whether or not it reaches a tipping point in which the majority of member states—including some of the wealthier and more influential countries such as Angola, Ethiopia, Kenya, Nigeria, and Sudan—become sufficiently democratic that they have nothing to fear by embracing stronger standards. If this happens, the growing consensus in favor of democratization would make it increasingly difficult for the continent's remaining authoritarian outposts to hold out. But this is only likely to occur if we see further reform at the domestic level—and as the last two chapters have demonstrated, this is far from certain.

# CONCLUSION: THE FUTURE OF FRAGILE AUTHORITARIANISM

How can this book help us to think about the future of authoritarianism in Africa? One of the main lessons of these pages has been that leaders have a number of ways in which they can sustain and legitimate authoritarian rule, but also that they are rarely more than an economic crisis or a series of bad economic decisions away from a popular uprising.

On the one hand, the ability to control information, use divide-and-rule tactics, and deploy the security forces can make it look like dictators hold all the cards. But as we saw in Chapter 1, authoritarianism often proves to have a remarkably fragile underbelly. Governments lack the resources they need to comfortably retain power, and citizens believe in the value of democratic rule—or at the very least, in the possibility that less repressive governments can generate both political and economic benefits. As a result, authoritarian leaders in countries such as Burkina Faso can lose control of the political agenda very quickly when things start to go against them.

In a sense, then, the main message of this book is to expect the unexpected. Authoritarian states that currently appear to be stable and durable, such as those in Angola, Cameroon, Ethiopia, and Rwanda, may be much more vulnerable than they currently appear. At the same time, the ability of leaders in some of the continent's more open political systems to draw on old authoritarian tropes and abuse their control over the security forces means that the future may bring periods of democratic backsliding in countries like Côte d'Ivoire, Tanzania, and Zambia. In other words, neither authoritarian reversal nor democratic consolidation can be assumed.

Indeed, recent trends suggest that in some respects it is actually getting easier to sustain authoritarian rule rather than harder. Consider some of the key factors that have been highlighted in this book. In Chapter 3, we described how strong economic foundations—in particular, the presence of valuable natural resources such as oil—enable authoritarian regimes to endure. Since the focus of that chapter in the 1970s, a host of new countries have located new, or greater, holdings natural resources. This includes significant finds of oil in Ghana, Kenya, and Uganda, potentially large offshore reserves in Namibia, and vast holdings of gas in Mozambique and Tanzania. As a result, the proportion of African states in which governments are empowered to negotiate with international partners and their citizens on their own terms has increased substantially over the last decade (see Image C.3).

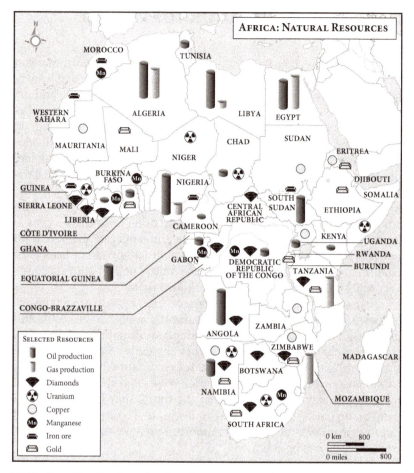

**MAP C.1** Distribution of national resources in Africa, 2019
*Source*: Based on "CSS Analysis (2008)", updated by the authors 2019.

At the same time, the increasingly complex international landscape means that there are more potential economic and political partners available for African leaders than ever before. In many ways this is a positive development, as it means that governments can choose to work with foreign states that align best with their favored political ethos and development strategies. But it also generates challenges for democratic consolidation. As we explored in Chapter 4, when African autocrats can play one foreign power off against another, as during the

Cold War, international pressure for leaders to respect political rights and civil liberties is least effective.

It is therefore significant that the value of Chinese trade with Africa has surpassed that of Europe and the United States. Furthermore, at the 2015 Forum on China-Africa Cooperation (FOCAC) meeting, China committed itself to US$60 billion of fresh investment in the shape of US$5 billion in grants, US$35 billion in concessional loans and export credits, $10 billion to set up a China-Africa Industrial Capacity Cooperation, and US$5 billion for the China-Africa Development Fund and a Special Loan for the Development of African Small- and Mid-Sized Enterprises. This is considerably more than the funds available to many of the countries that have typically put pressure on African states to democratize, such as the United Kingdom. While it is important not to demonize China (Brautigam 2009), which in many ways has been less destructive in its engagements with Africa that the Western countries described in Chapters 1 and 4, it is clear that its presence has transformed the international landscape in important ways.

Moreover, China is not alone. Over the last decade, Brazil, India, Iran, Israel, Russia, Saudi Arabia, South Korea, and Turkey have all become more prominent players. Although these states cannot come close to matching Chinese largesse, they nonetheless have the potential to reshape the options facing African leaders because, without exception, they are not interested in promoting democracy abroad. Either because they are authoritarian governments themselves, or because they do not prioritize exporting their own political model—as in the case of Brazil and India—these states do not demand that their partners demonstrate their democratic credentials.

Many Western governments have also lost the urge to advocate for democracy in Africa, compounding these global shifts. In Europe, the crisis generated by the decision of the United Kingdom to leave the European Union has deflected attention away from foreign policy concerns beyond Europe's borders. In the United States, the election of President Donald Trump, and his more insular focus on "making America great again," has led to a similar shift, with the US State Department reducing the emphasis that it places on promoting democracy abroad (Cheeseman and Klaas 2018).

While many of these trends are reversible, their combined impact has facilitated a marked decline in the quality of democracy in Africa over the last decade. According to Freedom House, the continent is in a democratic recession, with ten straight years of falling respect for political rights and civil liberties. From a peak in about 2006, there

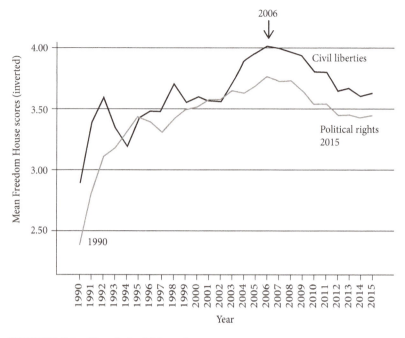

**FIGURE C.2** Trends in African democracy, 1990–2015.
*Source*: Bratton and Mattes (2016).

has been a consistent decline (see Figure C.2) ever since. However, to return to a constant theme of this study, this does not mean that authoritarian rule is destined to dominate the continent for years to come, because domestic forces will be just as significant in determining Africa's future as their international counterparts, if not more so.

At various points in this book we have documented the remarkable sacrifices made by African citizens to resist authoritarianism. Some of the factors that empower people to take back control over their own lives include education, free media, a strong civil society, and a coherent opposition. Significantly, there has also been significant movement in many of these areas over the last thirty years, and here things look more promising. The adult literacy rate in Africa increased from 53 percent in 1990 to 63 percent in 2015, and it is set to rise higher after a number of countries introduced free primary school education in the 1990s.

The spread of mobile phones, and of smartphones with Internet capacity, has also increased the ability of citizens to access information, multiplying the impact of greater education. In 2018, Africa achieved the fastest growth rate of Internet penetration in the world, with a 20 percent increase. While this growth has been uneven, and much less progress has been made in more closed economic and political systems, there is no question that it has increased the resources at the disposal of democratic activists. Especially following the emergence of platforms such as WhatsApp that allow users to share encrypted messages, there are new ways of coordinating opposition to dictatorship that did not exist in the 1980s.

Along with the potential for urbanization and the expansion of the middle class to generate more economically dependent and politically critical citizens, as discussed earlier in this chapter, this suggests that some of the factors that strengthen authoritarian regimes and embolden pro-democracy movements are growing in strength at the same time. The future is therefore unlikely to see a simple victory for democracy or authoritarianism, but rather a continuation of the struggle described in Chapters 4 and 5. Who will win out is likely to vary from country to country, depending on the ability of protestors to grow their coalitions by bridging ethnic and religious divides, and the capacity of authoritarian governments to attract new external partners, effectively manage the economy, and find ways to censor new technology so that they can consolidate their hold on power.

While there is no simple formula that can be applied to predict how these struggles will play out over the next two decades, one thing seems almost guaranteed: there will still be a need for books like this in twenty years' time.

## REFERENCES

Bratton, Michael, and Robert Mattes. "Do Africans Still Want Democracy?" *Afrobarometer Policy* Paper no. 36, 2016. http://afrobarometer.org/sites/default/files/publications/Policy%20papers/ab_r6_policypaperno36_do_africans_want_democracy.pdf.

Brautigam, Deborah. *The Dragon's Gift: The Real Story of China in Africa.* Oxford: Oxford University Press, 2009.

Cheeseman, Nic, and Brian Klaas. *How to Rig an Election.* New Haven, CT: Yale University Press, 2018.

CSS Analysis. "CSS Graphics: Natural Resources." 2008. http://www.css.ethz.ch/en/services/graphics/resources.html.

Gado Cartoons. "Cartoons." 2017. http://www.gadocartoons.com.

Gilpin, Caroline Crosson. "Teaching with 'The Rebel Puppeteers of Sudan.'" *New York Times*, October 20, 2017. https://www.nytimes.com/2017/10/20/learning/teaching-with-the-rebel-puppeteers-of-sudan.html.

Gogineni, Roopa. "The Rebel Puppeteers of Sudan." *New York Times*, October 3, 2017. https://www.nytimes.com/2017/10/03/opinion/the-rebel-puppeteers-of-sudan.html

Logan, Carolyn. "What Ails the Opposition in Africa?" Afrobarometer. 2015. http://www.afrobarometer.org/blogs/what-ails-opposition-africa.

Lungu, G. F. "The Church, Labour and the Press in Zambia: The Role of Critical Observers in a One-Party State." *African Affairs* 85, no. 340 (1986): 385–410.

Okumu, Wafula. "The African Union: Pitfalls and Prospects for Uniting Africa." *Journal of International Affairs* 62, no. 2 (2009): 93–111.

Riggan, Jennifer. *The Struggling State: Nationalism, Mass Militarization and the Education of Eritrea*. Philadelphia: Temple University Press, 2016.

## SUGGESTED READINGS

Bernal, Victoria. "'Please Forget Democracy and Justice': Eritrean Politics and the Power of Humour." *American Ethnologist* 40, no. 2 (2013): 300–309.

Bratton, Michael, Robert Mattes, and Emmanuel Gyimah-Boadi. *Public Opinion, Democracy, and Market Reform in Africa*. Cambridge: Cambridge University Press, 2005.

Eko, Lyombe. "The Art of Criticism: How African Cartoons Discursively Constructed African Media Realities in the Post-Cold War Era." *Critical African Studies* 2, no. 4 (2012): 65–91.

Gagliardone, Iginio. *The Politics of Technology in Africa: Communication, Development, and Nation-Building in Ethiopia*. New York: Cambridge University Press, 2016.

Njogu, Kimani, and Hervé Maupeu, eds. *Songs and Politics in Eastern Africa*. Oxford: African Books Collective, 2007.

Stremlau, Nicole. "The Press and the Political Restructuring of Ethiopia." *Journal of Eastern African Studies* 5, no. 4 (2012): 716–32.

wa Thiong'o, Ngũgĩ. *Penpoints, Gunpoints, and Dreams: Towards a Critical Theory of the Arts and the State in Africa*. Oxford: Oxford University Press, 1998.

Willems, Wendy. "Comic Strips and 'the Crisis': Postcolonial Laughter and Coping with Everyday Life in Zimbabwe." *Popular Communication* 9, no. 2 (2011): 126–45.

# Key Terms and Concepts

**Absolute monarchy:** An absolute monarchy is a form of rule where a ruler has "absolute" authority and where their power is not—in theory and/or in practice—limited by laws or other political actors. A famous historical example of absolute monarchy is France under the Bourbon dynasty (particularly King Louis XIV, who reigned from 1643 to 1715), though a number of states are governed in this manner today. Eswatini (formerly Swaziland) is the only formal example of absolute monarchy in contemporary Africa, but the term has been used informally to refer to the "sultanistic" regimes (see Introduction) of nonroyal rulers such as Mobutu Sese Seko of Zaire (in power from 1965 to 1997). Jean-Bedel Bokasa of Central African Republic was also briefly an absolute monarch after declaring himself "Emperor of Central Africa" in 1976, though his elevation was not recognized by foreign governments.

**Africanization:** Literally meaning "to make African," Africanization refers to a set of processes or policies which have as their goal the replacement of putatively non-African institutions, norms, personnel, names, and identities with their African equivalents. The term is often used to describe the reform of colonial governing institutions undertaken across Africa in the postindependence era (largely the 1960s and 1970s) whereby a range of policies and practices (including, in some cases, affirmative action) were introduced by African governments to replace white, colonial administrators with African officials. "Africanizing" states and societies on the continent more generally has also been a political and ideological agenda for a number of authoritarian African leaders, as Chapter 2 demonstrates. The *retour à l'authenticité* (return to authenticity) governing ideology of President Mobutu Sese Seko of Zaire (in power 1965–1997), for example, dictated the changing of "European" names—of people, streets, towns, rivers, and even the country itself—to reflect precolonial "African" identities and the promulgation of strict rules effecting many aspects of everyday life, including the banning of "European" clothes such as suits.

**Arab Spring:** A series of protests and demonstrations against authoritarian governments in North Africa and the Middle East initiated in 2011 which led to civil war (in Libya, Syria, and Yemen), external intervention (in Bahrain, Libya, Syria, and Yemen), political reform, and the resignation or removal of a range of authoritarian rulers and governments (in Egypt, Libya, Tunisia, and Yemen).

**Authoritarianism:** Authoritarian systems of government are those in which the leader is not selected through *free and fair* elections, but rather relies on force to remain in power. There are a great variety of authoritarian political systems in Africa, which use different levels of violence and intimidation. A very small number do not hold elections. Most hold elections, but under highly repressive conditions (often known as competitive-authoritarian systems).

**Big-man politics/big men:** Often used to describe **patronage-based** politics (see later), "big man politics" refers to a political system where politicians maintain power through distributing—both state and personal—resources to chains of "clients" stretching from the national level to the local. In return, the politicians in question can rely on "clients" to mobilize support for them in particular regions and within particular communities. In Africa, the dominant personalities in these chains of patronage have traditionally been male, though in many countries female politicians are now increasingly central (see Chapter 5). The concept continues to have analytical purchase among scholars, though, in spite of this misnomer.

**Chief:** This term usually refers to a leader of an ethnic group or clan whose authority was historically based on lineage or descent rather than merit or election. Sometimes the institution of chieftaincy is referred to in other terms, such as "traditional leadership."

**Collectivization of economic production:** The consolidation of individual labor and landholdings (particularly agricultural) into collective entities by the state. This was a key economic policy of the USSR during the 1930s and formed a core part of Josef Stalin's famous first "five-year plan." The approach has since been adopted by a range of socialist governments, including those in Africa.

**Conditionality:** The act of placing political or economic conditions on the provision of assistance of one kind or another. In the African context, the term is usually used in relation to the conditions imposed by international aid donors, the International Monetary Fund, and the World Bank in order for states to secure economic and loans.

**Coup:** A takeover of power by the military, in which the former government is overthrown by force.

**Deputy:** The equivalent of a Member of Parliament in the French National Assembly.

**Developmental:** A government, party, or leader committed to and (more or less) successful at providing development. This may refer to economic growth, the development of a national infrastructure, jobs, or public services such as health and education.

**Feudal system:** Broadly speaking, a form of political system and set of reciprocal relationships whereby landholders permit peasants to hold and work their land in return for rents, surplus, loyalty, and—when requested—military assistance. This was the prevailing system of political authority within medieval Europe and in imperial Ethiopia.

**Hybrid system:** In political science, a hybrid political system is one where two or more systems of rule are merged or interact closely within the same system. Many authoritarian African states are "hybridized" in that they are ruled through a mix of two systems—a formal, rule-based bureaucratic system and an informal, personalized, and unpredictable system (see Introduction).

**Illiberal state-building:** The process of building a state's capacity using authoritarian strategies rather than democratic ones.

**Karl Marx, Friedrich Engels, and Vladimir Lenin:** Marx and Engels were German political philosophers who developed the core theories of revolutionary socialism in a series of publications including *The Communist Manifesto* (Marx and Engels 1848) and *Das Kapital* (Marx 1867). Lenin, deeply influenced by these theories, was active in revolutionary politics in early twentieth-century imperial Russia, ultimately becoming a leading figure in the October 1917 Russian Revolution and the Russian leader between 1917 and 1924. Marx, Engels, and Lenin have traditionally been venerated in socialist states, including in *Derg*-ruled Ethiopia.

**Multiparty politics:** A type of political system in which multiple parties are allowed to operate and compete for power through elections. Modern-day democracies employ a form of multiparty politics.

**Neo-patrimonialism:** A theoretical framework for understanding the practice of politics in Africa from the colonial era onward. Whereas "patrimonialism" is taken to refer to traditional forms of government, the term "neo-patrimonialism" is intended to signify that following the imposition of the colonial state African political systems can no longer be treated as purely traditional. The reason for this is that patrimonial modes of conducting politics were grafted onto the trappings of the modern state, including political parties, legislatures, and judiciaries. In the process, both patrimonial and formal institutional structures were transformed.

**One-party state:** A type of government in which only one political party— the ruling party—is allowed to operate and so people are denied the ability to select their leader or determine national party. However, in Africa, many one-party states did hold elections that allowed citizens to select their local representatives from a list of candidates approved by the party.

**Patrimonialism:** A theoretical framework for understanding the practice of politics in some societies. Taken literally, patrimonialism simply means "of or from one's ancestors." The term was popularized by Max Weber, who used it to refer to a traditional form of domination, that is, a system of government in which authority derives not from elections or the merit of candidates but from another source, such as the fact that they are born into a particular family or group, as in a monarchy.

**Patronage-based system:** Patronage-based, or patron–client, systems are argued by many scholars to be at the heart of many African states. The relationship between patronage and authoritarianism is explored in

Chapters 1 and 3 in particular and refers to a form of rule based around rulers "buying" or "renting" support from chains of subordinates ("clients"). The resources provided by "patrons" come in many forms and can be domestic (natural resources, preferential access to contracts and deals, cash, etc.) and international (development aid) in origin.

**Regime maintenance:** A political science term which refers to how a state or government sustains itself in power. Regime maintenance strategies in authoritarian states have usually combined both coercive and patronage-based approaches, along with reliance upon core ideas of legitimate rule and international support networks (see Chapter 4).

**Sectarianism:** An intense allegiance to a particular identity, usually religious or ethnic, which places emphasis on the demonization of alternative, rival identities—often leading to violence when played out in the political sphere. Sectarianism has been a key propaganda target of African authoritarian leaders who have sought to legitimize themselves as guarantors of "national unity" in the face of internal divisions.

**State:** The overarching legal, constitutional, and economic framework in a given country. "State" is often used as a blanket term to refer to both to the way that power is exercised and the permanent institutions of a country, including the bureaucracy and the security forces. While the government in charge may change regularly (for example, at every election), the state often remains the same for long periods of time.

**State capacity:** The ability of a state to carry out its key functions. These are usually thought to include the ability to collect taxes, enforce the rule of law, deliver services, and defend itself against attack.

**Structural adjustment program** (s): Conditions attached to loans provided by the World Bank and International Monetary Fund (IMF) to countries experiencing economic instability. The term is commonly used to describe conditions applied to loans during the 1980s in particular, which aimed at reducing the size of the state and stimulating the private sector. Specific policy conditions in this regard have included the privatization of state assets and companies, rolling back economic regulations and cutting the number of civil servants ("retrenchment"). Structural adjustment programs have generally been considered not only to have been unsuccessful but also damaging since they led to a significant reduction in state spending—in Africa and beyond—on health, education, and other core areas of the social sector.

**Surveillance state:** A surveillance state is a concept used to describe a state which rules through constantly monitoring and tracking the activities of its citizens—today increasingly through the Internet and social media—often using information obtained to crack down on perceived opponents or limit the influence of perceived critics. There is growing evidence of authoritarian African states using surveillance technologies to shut down opposition communications in the lead-up to and during elections, though many Western states are also referred to as "surveillance states" by analysts.

# Index

*Boxes, figures, maps, notes, and tables are indicated by b, f, m, n, and t following the page number. Images are indicated by italicized page numbers. Surnames starting with "al" are alphabetized by the subsequent part of the name.*

## A

Abacha, Sani, 52*b*, 53
absolute monarchy, xxvi, 20
Africa. *See also specific countries*
  chieftaincy in (*see* chiefs)
  Cold War in (*see* Cold War)
  colonial period in (*see* colonialism)
  communism in, 61–62, 67–70, 68*b*, 78
  democratic trends in, 127–128, 128*f*
  economy in (*see* economy)
  emancipatory movements in, 121
  Freedom House rankings for, 48, 49*t*, 90,
    127–128, 128*f*
  gatekeeper states in, 48, 52*b*, 57
  legislative representation of women in,
    98–100*b*, 102
  literacy rates in, 128
  location of capital cities in, 6*m*
  longest-serving leaders in, xix*b*
  natural resource distribution in, 125, 126*m*
  public attitudes toward democracy in,
    108–112, 110*f*
  third wave of democratization in, xix
  women in parliament in, 98–100*b*, 102
African democracy, 100, 100–101*b*, 111
Africanization, 7, 32–35, 42, 100
African National Congress (ANC), 35, 36,
  37–40*b*, 41, 42
African Peer Review Mechanism (APRM),
  121, 123
African Renaissance, 121
African Union (AU), xviii, 119, 121–124,
  122–123*b*
Afrobarometer, 108–111, 108n1
Afwerki, Isaias, xix*b*
Ahidjio, Ahmadou, 32, 33*b*
aid. *See* foreign aid
Albaih, Khalid, 117
Amha Selassie, 19

Amin, Idi, xxvi, 28, 33*b*, 69, 77*b*, 104
Amnesty International, 83, 85
ANC. *See* African National Congress
Anderson, David M., 8, 31
Angola
  colonial rule in, 11*b*
  foreign aid to, 69*b*
  illiberal state-building activities in, 46
  Iraq War supported by, 79
  oil industry in, xxi, 46, 48
  settler colonialism in, 8*b*
  stability of authoritarian regime in, 125
  state capacity of, xxi
apartheid, 16, 22, 35–36, 41, 42
APRM (African Peer Review Mechanism),
  121, 123
Arab Spring, 108
Arendt, Hannah, xxvi
*arpillera* (patchwork), 114–115, *115*
Ashanti Kingdom, 9
assimilation, 10*b*
AU. *See* African Union
authoritarianism. *See also specific countries*
  afterlives of deposed leaders, 76–77*b*
  artistic and cultural critiques of, 114–115, *115*
  colonial rule and predisposition to, 4–5, 7–9
  conceptualizations of, xxv–xxviii
  degrees of, xxiv*b*, xxvi
  democracy vs., 97–98, 100–104
  developmental, 90–94, 96
  dictatorships (*see* dictatorships)
  economy and (*see* economy)
  electoral, xxiv*b*, 86–90, 87*t*
  everyday experiences with, 113–118
  foreign aid and (*see* foreign aid)
  fragile, 5, 14, 16–17, 59, 125–129
  future of, 125–129
  humor as means of expression under,
    115–118, *116*

authoritarianism (*continued*)
  hybrid systems of, xxvii
  legislative representation of women in, 98–100*b*
  maintenance of (*see* regime maintenance)
  military regimes (*see* military regimes)
  one-party rule (*see* one-party states)
  power of ideas in, 29–35
  precolonial traditions used in, 20–21, 29–30, 33–34
  resilience of, xviii–xix, 21, 66, 118–120
  titles and honorifics for leaders, 32, 33–34*b*
  typologies in postindependence era, 21–25, 22*t*, 28–29
  violence and (*see* violence)
  white minority governments, 22, 35, 53–54, 68*b*
Awolowo, Obafemi, 15
Awori, Aggrey, 15
Awori, Moody, 15
Ayittey, George, 97, 101

**B**
Bah, Samba, xxiii*b*
Banda, Hastings Kamuzu
  Africanization efforts of, 33
  end of rule of, 66, 75, 76*b*
  feelings of betrayal, 79
  human rights record, 24
  international criticisms of, 74
  legitimizing narratives used by, 31
  regime maintenance efforts, xx, 25
  titles used by, 34*b*
  western influences on, 42, 43
Banda, Joyce, 123
Barre, Siad, 61–62
Barrow, Adama, xviii
al-Bashir, Omar, xix*b*, 117
Bauer, Gretchen, 99*b*
Bayart, Jean-François, 79
Belgium, colonial rule by, 11*b*, 91
Benin
  colonial rule in, 10*b*
  military regimes in, 29
  multiparty politics in, 71, 76, 76*b*
  as one-party state, 30, 70
Berlin Wall, fall of (1989), 65, 70
big-men politics
  categorization of rulers in, xxvi
  in colonial period, 5, 13–17
  corruption in, 103
  in divide-and-rule strategies, 88
  fragility of, 77*b*
  origins of term, 13

  political machines in, xx
Biti, Tendai, 120
Biya, Paul, xix*b*, 32, 82, 83, 104, 124
Bokassa, Jean-Bédel, xxvi, 23*b*, 29, 33*b*, 70
Bongo, Omar, 104
Booth, David, 103
Bopape, David, 36
Botswana
  democracy in, 5
  economic growth in, 90
Bratton, Michael, 108
Brazil, engagement with African states, 127
Buhari, Muhammadu, 76
Burkina Faso, popular uprisings in, 107, 108
Burnet, Jennie, 99*b*
Burundi
  female leadership in, 23–24*b*
  legislative representation of women in, 99*b*
Bush, George W., 79

**C**
Camara, Juma K., xxii*b*
Cameroon
  colonial rule in, 10*b*
  democratic backsliding in, 124
  economic independence from foreign aid, 120
  legitimizing narratives in, 32
  multiparty politics in, 82–83
  oil industry in, 48
  stability of authoritarian regime in, 125
  suppression of dissent in, 82–83
CAR. *See* Central African Republic
Carnation Revolution (1974), 11*b*
Carter, Jimmy, 62
"The Carter Cables," 62, 63–65*b*
Carville, James, 48n2
Ceesay, Fatou, xxii*b*
censorship, 4, 75, 82, 129
Central African Republic (CAR)
  dictatorship in, 29
  female leadership in, 23*b*, 24*b*
  legislative representation of women in, 102
  sultanism in, xxvi
Césaire, Aimé, 12*b*
Chad
  colonial rule in, 10*b*
  oil industry in, 48
  persistence of authoritarianism in, xx
  state capacity of, xxi
Chalker, Lynda, 72*b*
Chama Cha Mapinduzi, 30, 77*b*
Chamisa, Nelson, 120
Cheibub, Jose Antonio, 46

chiefs
    in authoritarian systems, 21, 33
    colonial-era powers of, 3*b*, 10, 12–13
    defined, 3*b*
    in patronage-based systems, xx
    in policy formation, 97, 101–102
    subordination to political control, 3
Chiluba, Frederick, 74
China
    economic growth in, 113
    foreign aid from, xxi, 69*b*, 80
    global rise of, 85, 97
    role in authoritarian revival, 102
    trade with Africa, 53, 127
Chiwenga, Constantino, 119
civil wars, 14, 24*b*, 30, 46, 59, 69*b*
clientelism, xxix, 46
Cold War, xxi, 26*b*, 61–70, 63–65*b*, 68–69*b*
collectivization of economic production, 30
colonialism, 3–17
    African responses to, 12–13*b*
    big-men politics during, 5, 13–17
    chiefs and traditional leaders in, 3*b*, 10,
        12–13
    economy during, 5, 8*b*, 10–11*b*, 13
    education during, 7, 43
    as fragile authoritarianism, 16–17
    legacy of, 5–9, 8*b*, 14–15, 66–67
    predisposition to authoritarianism due to,
        4–5, 7–9
    resistance to, xviii, 7–8
    settler colonialism, 8*b*, 22
    social consequences of, 5
    variations of, 10–11*b*
communism, 61–62, 67–70, 68*b*, 78
Compaoré, Blaise, 107, 108
conditionality, 66, 70–75, 72*b*
Congo. *See* Democratic Republic of Congo
consensual democracy, 112
containment policy, 68, 68–69*b*
Convention People's Party (CPP), 1, 3–4, 43
Cooper, Fred, 48
copper industry, 54–55
corruption
    in big-men politics, 103
    criticisms of, 41
    depiction through cartoons, 116
    in elections, xvii–xix, 66, 73, 82–90, 87*t*
    foreign aid and, 69
    in gatekeeper states, 52*b*, 57
    good governance model on, 71
    in military regimes, 25, 51
    reduction of, 85, 90, 92, 103
Cote d'Ivoire

democratic backsliding in, 125
oil industry in, 48
coups. *See also* military regimes
    commemoration of, xxii*b*
    communist-inspired, 61
    condemnation by African Union, 123, 124
    international support for, 25–26*b*, 70
    justification for, 25, 26*b*
    postcolonial, xvii, 4, 25–27*b*
CPP (Convention People's Party), 1, 3–4, 43
Cuba, legislative representation of
    women in, 99*b*

**D**

Dacko, David, 23*b*, 29
Dawit Isaac, 118
Dawit Wolde Giorgis, 20
Déby, Idris, xix*b*
Decker, Alicia, 28
Defiance Campaign Against Unjust Laws, 36
democracy. *See also* multiparty politics
    African, 100, 100–101*b*, 111
    authoritarianism vs., 97–98, 100–104
    backsliding from, 124, 125
    barriers to democratization, 4–5
    in colonial period, 9
    conceptualizations of, 86
    consensual, 112
    European Council Resolution on, 72*b*
    fragments in one-party states, 23
    legislative representation of women in, 98*b*
    liberal, 66, 71, 71n8
    no-party democracy, xxiv, 31
    promotion of, xxi, 71, 127
    public attitudes toward, 108–112, 110*f*
    third wave of democratization, xix
    trends in Africa, 127–128, 128*f*
Democratic Republic of Congo (DRC)
    Africanization in, 34
    civil war in, 59
    colonial rule in, 11*b*
    corruption in, 52*b*
    dictatorship in, 24–25, 29
    foreign aid to, 68
    legislative representation of women in, 102
    legitimation of authoritarian rule in, 21
    national conferences held in, 71
    oil industry in, 48
    state capacity of, xxi
deputies, in French National Assembly, 10*b*, 43
*Derg* regime, 19, 21, 68, 69
developmental authoritarianism, 90–94, 96
developmental partnerships, xxi, 85
developmental patrimonialism, 103

development assistance. *See* foreign aid
dictatorships. *See also* one-party states;
    *specific countries*
    conceptualizations of, xxvi, 29
    features of, xvii
    human rights in, 24–25
Diogo, Luísa, 23*b*
Diop, Cheikh Anta, 121
disabled persons, equal rights for, 98
discrimination
    apartheid, 16, 22, 35–36, 41, 42
    political opposition and, 90
    racism, 8*b*, 10*b*, 13
    sexism, 13
    white supremacy, 35
divide-and-rule strategies, 75, 87*t*, 88–89, 91, 125
Djibouti
    economic growth in, 90, 91*f*
    legislative representation of women in, 102
domino theory, 67–68
Domitien, Elisabeth, 23*b*
dos Santos, Isabel, 45, 46
dos Santos, José Eduardo, 45, 107
DRC. *See* Democratic Republic of Congo

**E**
Economic Community of West African States
    (ECOWAS), 24*b*
economic equality, 36, 37*b*, 41, 42
economy, 45–59. *See also* oil industry
    in apartheid, 35–36
    collectivization of production in, 30
    in colonial period, 5, 8*b*, 10–11*b*, 13
    copper industry, 54–55
    developmental authoritarianism and,
        90–94, 96
    as driver of election outcomes, 48
    in gatekeeper states, 48, 52*b*, 57
    GDP per capita, 55–56, 56*f*
    management of, 90, 93
    marginalized groups in, 28
    natural resources impacting, 57, 59
    patronage-based systems in, 46, 51
    political stability and, 46–47
    structural adjustment programs, 55
    world's fast growing economies, 90, 91*f*
ECOWAS (Economic Community of West
    African States), 24*b*
education
    during apartheid, 36
    in colonial period, 7, 43
    Freedom Charter on, 39*b*
    literacy rates and, 128
    political, 111, 112*b*
    support for democracy and, 109

unity promoted through, 30
elections. *See also* multiparty politics
    ballot example, 73, 73*f*
    checks and balances for, 1, 86
    in colonial period, 7, 9
    corruption in, xvii–xix, 66, 73, 82–90, 87*t*
    democratic legitimacy through, 47
    drivers of outcomes in, 48
    good governance model on, 71
    vulnerability of, 86
electoral authoritarianism, xxiv*b*,
        86–90, 87*t*
Engels, Friedrich, 20
equality
    economic, 36, 37*b*, 41, 42
    Freedom Charter on, 42
    gender, 98, 98–100*b*, 102
Equatorial Guinea
    legislative representation of women in, 98*b*
    oil industry in, xxi, 48
    state capacity of, xxi
Eritrea
    foreign aid to, 80
    humor as means of expression in, 117–118
    Iraq War supported by, 79
    legislative representation of women in, 102
    media sources in, 114
    nationalism in, xxiii
    as one-party state, 66
Eswatini
    legislative representation of women in, 102
    public attitudes toward democracy in, 109
Ethiopia
    Imperial monarchy of, 19
    *Derg* regime in, 19, 21, 68, 69
    economic growth in, 90, 91*f*, 97, 113
    feudal system in, 19–20
    foreign aid to, 68
    Iraq War supported by, 79
    legitimizing narratives in, xxii, xxiii, 93
    socialism in, 19–20, 62
    stability of authoritarian regime in, 125
    state capacity of, xxi
ethnic groups.
    border determinations impacting, 14–15
    chiefs and traditional leaders of, 3*b*, 9, 13
    competition for power among, 14
    conflicts between, 88–89, 91–92
    Apartheid South Africa homeland creation
        for, 36
    neo-patrimonialism and, 15, 51
European Council Resolution on Human
    Rights, Democracy and Development
    (1991), 72*b*
Eyadéma, Gnassingbé, 66

**F**
Falola, Toyin, 30, 41–42
females. *See* women
femocracy, 99*b*
feudal system, 19–20
Foa, Roberto, 90, 102, 103
FORD (Forum for the Restoration of
    Democracy), 88–89
foreign aid, 61–80
    "The Carter Cables," 62, 63–65*b*
    during Cold War, xxi, 61, 62, 66–70,
        68–69*b*
    conditionality and, 66, 70–75, 72*b*
    corruption involving, 69
    critical approaches to, 80
    developmental partnerships and, xxi, 85
    donor recommendations for, 78–79
    economic growth due to, 93
    economic independence from, 120
    for gatekeeper states, 48
    multiparty politics promoted through, 66,
        75, 84, 88
    structural adjustment programs, 55
Forum for the Restoration of Democracy
    (FORD), 88–89
fragile authoritarianism, 5, 14, 16–17, 59,
    125–129
France
    colonial rule by, 10–11*b*, 67
    coups supported by, 25–26*b*
    foreign aid from, xxi
    on political conditionality, 72*b*
Freedom Charter, 35, 36, 37–40*b*, 42
Freedom House rankings, 48, 49*t*, 90,
    127–128, 128*f*
Freund, Bill, 10
Fukuyama, Francis, 71n8

**G**
Gabon
    national conferences held in, 71
    oil industry in, xxi, 48
    state capacity of, xxi
Gallagher, Julia, 48
The Gambia, presidential election in (2016),
    xvii–xviii, 107
Ganja (artist), 117
gatekeeper states, 48, 52*b*, 57
Gbagbo, Laurent, 77*b*
Gbeho, Philip Comi, 2–3*b*
Geddes, Barbara, xxvii–xxviii
gender equality, 98, 98–100*b*, 102
genocide, xxiv*b*, 66, 78, 92, 93
Ghana
    chiefs and traditional leaders in, 3, 3*b*

colonial rule in, 10–11*b*
independence of, 1
legitimizing narratives in, xxiii
military regimes in, 4, 28
national anthem of, 1, 2–3*b*
oil finds in, 125
Global War on Terror, 62, 79
Golooba-Mutebi, Frederick, 103
good governance, 47, 71, 94, 121
Guinea, independence of, 32, 67

**H**
Haber, Stephen, xxvii
Habyarimana, Juvénal, 91, 92
Haile Selassie I (Ethiopia), 19, 20, 25*b*–26*b*,
    62, 70, 76*b*
Hempstone, Smith, 72*b*
Herbst, Jeffrey, 21
Hitchens, Christopher, xxvi
human rights
    African Union on, 122*b*
    in dictatorships, 24–25
    European Council Resolution on, 72*b*
    Freedom Charter on, 39*b*
    genocide and, xxiv*b*, 66, 78, 92, 93
    good governance model on, 71
    International Criminal Court and, 77*b*
    in military regimes, 51, 53
    in one-party states, 24
    violation of, xviii, 11*b*, 51, 83–85, 89, 120
humor, as means of expression, 115–118, *116*
Hun Sen, xix*b*
Hurd, Douglas, 72*b*
Hutu community, 91–92
hybrid systems, xxvii

**I**
Igbo communities, 9–10, 12
illiberal state-building activities, 46
India
    economic growth in, 90, 91*f*
    engagement with African states, 127
indirect rule, 11*b*
international assistance. *See* foreign aid
International Criminal Court, 77*b*, 121
International Monetary Fund, 55, 56, 74
Internet access, 117, 120, 128–129
Iraq War, 79

**J**
Jackson, Robert, xxvi, 83
Jammeh, Yahya, xvii–xviii, xxii–xxiii*b*, 77*b*,
    107, 124
Jawara, Dawda, xvii
Joseph, Richard, 51

**K**

Kadzamira, Cecilia, 25
Kagame, Paul, 16, 80, 91–94, 99–101*b*
Kamuzu Academy, 42, 42n1
KANU (Kenya African National Union), 31,
 74, 77*b*
Kasa-Vubu, Joseph, 26*b*
Kaunda, Kenneth
 ballots used for, 73, 73*f*
 economic challenges faced by, 53, 55, 56
 end of rule of, 66, 86
 foreign aid and, 69*b*, 74
 justification for one-party state, 24
Kenya
 colonial rule in, 8*b*, 9, 10–11*b*, 13
 economic independence from foreign aid,
  120–121
 foreign aid to, 74–75
 freedom movement in, 40–41
 humor as means of expression in,
  115–117, *116*
 multiparty politics in, 75, 87–89
 nationalism in, xxiii
 oil finds in, 125
 as one-party state, 30
 settler colonialism in, 8*b*
 suppression of dissent in, 89
Kenya African National Union (KANU), 31,
 74, 77*b*
Kenyatta, Jomo, 32, 33, 34*b*, 40, 43
Kenyatta, "Mama" Ngina, 32
Kenyatta, Uhuru, 32, 116
Kérékou, Mathieu, 66, 70–71, 76, 86
Khameini, Ali, xix*b*
Kinigi, Sylvie, 23–24*b*

**L**

labeling, 103–104
labor unions. *See* trade unions
Laos, economic growth in, 90, 91*f*
Larmer, Miles, 55
legitimizing narratives, xxii–xxv, 31, 32,
 85, 93–94
Lenin, Vladimir, 20, 78
Leopold II (Belgium), 11*b*
LGBTQ+ Rights, 102
liberal democracy, 66, 71, 71n8
Liberia
 civil war in, 24*b*
 female leadership in, 24*b*
Linz, Juan, xxvi
Londsale, John, 7
Lozi Kingdom, 9
Lugard, Frederick, 11*b*
Lumumba, Patrice, 25*b*

**M**

Macías Nguema, Francisco, 28, 70, 76*b*
Madagascar, public attitudes toward
 democracy in, 109
Magaloni, Beatriz, xxviii
Malawi
 African Union pressure on, 123
 dictatorship in, 24–25, 29
 foreign aid to, 74–75
 Kamuzu Academy, 42, 42n1
 multiparty politics in, 75
 nationalism in, xxiii
 oil imports in, 53
 persistence of authoritarianism in, xx
 public attitudes toward democracy in, 109
 state capacity of, xxi
Malawi Congress Party, 74, 77*b*
Mali
 legitimizing narratives in, xxiii
 national conferences held in, 71
Mama, Amina, 99*b*
Mandela, Nelson, 36, 41
Mao Zedong, 78
Marx, Karl, 20, 78
Masaki, Takaaki, 103
Matiba, Kenneth, 88–89
Mattes, Robert, 108
Mauritania, suspension from African Union, 123
Mauritius
 democracy in, 5
 economic growth in, 90
Mbayo, Esther, 96*b*
Mbeki, Thabo, 121
MDC (Movement for Democratic Change),
 118–120
Meles (Zenawi), 94
Menelik II (Ethiopia), 20
Mengistu Hailemariam, 19–21, 77*b*
military regimes. *See also* coups; *specific
  countries*
 corruption in, 25, 51
 decline of, 83
 fragile authoritarianism and, 5
 human rights issues in, 51, 53
 international response to, 53
 one-party states formed from, 29
 political rights in, xxviii, 30–31
 violence in, 28
Mitterrand, François, 72*b*
MMD (Movement for Multi-party
 Democracy), 74
Mnangagwa, Emmerson, 119, 120
Mobutu Seso Seko (Joseph-Désiré Mobutu)
 Africanization efforts of, 34
 corruption of, 52*b*, 69

human rights record, 24
justification for one-party states, 35
as regional force for stability, 66, 78
rise to power, 25, 26*b*, 29
titles used by, 33*b*
western influences on, 42
Moi, Daniel arap
Africanization efforts of, 33
coup attempt against, 40
election rigging by, 66, 87–89
international criticisms of, 74
on multiparty politics, xxiv, 75
titles used by, 34*b*
torture as tactic used by, 41
Movement for Democratic Change (MDC),
118–120
Movement for Multi-party Democracy
(MMD), 74
Movement System, 31
Moyo, Sibusiso, 26*b*
Mozambique
colonial rule in, 11*b*
female leadership in, 23*b*
foreign aid to, 66, 69*b*, 78–79
natural gas reserves in, 125
settler colonialism in, 8*b*
MPLA (People's Movement for the Liberation
of Angola), 46
Mugabe, Robert, 26*b*, 77*b*, 104, 108, 114,
118–120, 124
multiparty politics. *See also* democracy;
elections
authoritarian subversion of, xix, 53, 71
criticisms of, xxiv, 30
foreign aid in promotion of, 66, 75, 84, 88
introduction of, 53, 56, 57, 71, 82
political rights and, xxviii
Muluzi, Bakili, 75
Museveni, Yoweri
foreign aid strategy of, 78
on LGBTQ+ Rights, 102
legitimization of political system by, 93–94
number of years in power, xix*b*
poem in praise of, 94–96*b*
on post-Cold War era, xxi, 70
progressive legislation of, 98
Mutharika, Bingu wa, 123
*Mwakenya* movement, 41
Mwampembwa, Godfrey "Gado," *116*, 116–118

**N**
Namibia
oil finds in, 125
public attitudes toward democracy in, 109
settler colonialism in, 8*b*, 22

nationalism, xxiii, 6, 11*b*, 31, 61. *See also* unity
National Party (NP), 22, 35–36, 41
National Resistance Movement, 30–31, 78,
94, 94*b*
natural resources, 5–6, 47, 57, 59, 125, 126*m*.
*See also specific resources*
Nazarbayev, Nursultan, xix*b*
Négritude movement, 12–13*b*
neo-patrimonialism, 15, 51, 103
New Partnership for Africa's Development
(NEPAD), 121
Nigeria
civil war in, 30
colonial rule in, 9, 10–11*b*
corruption in, 51, 52*b*, 57
geo-strategic importance of, 51
Igbo communities of, 9–10, 12
legitimizing narratives in, xxiii
military regimes in, 28, 51, 53
multiparty politics in, 57, 76, 76*b*
oil industry in, xxi, 48–51, 53, 54, 57
population of, 54n4
state capacity of, xxi
9/11 terrorist attacks (2001), 79
Nkrumah, Kwame, xxvi, 1, 4, 25*b*, 33*b*, 42–43
no-party democracy, xxiv, 31
NP (National Party), 22, 35–36, 41
Ntaryamira, Cyprien, 92
Nyerere, Julius
Africanization efforts of, 33
on common good, 111
on education, 112*b*
foreign aid and, 69*b*
political participation allowed by, 24
power relinquished by, 76*b*
titles used by, 33*b*
*ujamaa* philosophy of, 30

**O**
OAU (Organization of African Unity), 121, 122*b*
Obasanjo, Olusegun, 76, 121
Obiang Nguema Mbasogo, Teodoro, xix*b*, 28
Obote, Milton, 25*b*, 70, 77*b*
Odinga, Oginga, 89
Odinga, Raila, 116
oil industry
exploitation of workers in, 54
government revenue from, xxi, 46,
51, 53, 57
new finds in, 125
OPEC and, 50
political freedom and, 48, 49*t*
price shocks in, 46, 56
value of crude oil, 49, 50*f*
Okuson, Sonny, 58*b*

one-party states. *See also* dictatorships; *specific countries*
  decline of, xviii, 66, 83, 84
  economic issues in, 55–56
  formation from military regimes, 29
  fragile authoritarianism and, 5
  fragments of democracy in, 23
  human rights in, 24
  legitimacy of, 22–24
  nationalist ideals in, xxiii, 31, 61
  negotiation processes in, 55
  political education in, 111
  political rights in, xxviii, 24, 73
  unity in, xxiii, 30–31, 34–35, 101
Organization of African Unity (OAU), 121, 122*b*
Organization of the Petroleum Exporting Countries (OPEC), 50
Ouko, Robert, 74

**P**
patrimonialism, 15, 51, 103
patronage-based systems, xviii, xx, 46, 51
People's Movement for the Liberation of Angola (MPLA), 46
Pereira, Carmen, 23*b*
Perry, Ruth, 24*b*
personal rule. *See* dictatorships
petro-states, 46, 57, 58*b*
political bargaining, 55
political conditionality, 66, 70–75, 72*b*
political education, 111, 112*b*
political violence, 8*b*, 14, 75, 114–115, 120
Portugal, colonial rule by, 11*b*
poverty, 67, 85, 90, 93, 111, 113
praise songs, xxii–xxiii*b*, xxv
prebendalism, 51, 55
propaganda, xxiv–xxv, 32, 87*t*, 88, 111

**Q**
*Qey Shibir* (Ethiopian Red Terror), 21, 69

**R**
racism, 8*b*, 10*b*, 13
Rahmon, Emomali, xix*b*
Red Terror, Ethiopian (*Qey Shibir*) 21, 69
  regime maintenance
  foreign aid and (*see* foreign aid)
  government revenue for, xx–xxi, 47–48, 51
  legitimizing narratives in, xxii–xxv, 31, 32, 85, 93–94
  political machines in, xx
  in post-Cold War era, 75–76
  propaganda in, xxiv–xxv, 32, 87*t*, 88, 111
  security mechanisms for, xx, 25

"Revolutionary Presidents" (poem), 94–96*b*
Rhodesia. *See* Zimbabwe
Riggan, Jennifer, 117–118
Rosberg, Carl, xxvi
Rwanda
  African democracy in, 100–101*b*
  economic growth in, 90–93, 97, 103, 113
  economic independence from foreign aid, 120
  female leadership in, 23–24*b*
  foreign aid to, 80, 93
  genocide in, 66, 78, 92, 93
  invasion from Uganda, 91
  Iraq War supported by, 79
  legislative representation of women in, 99*b*
  legitimizing narratives in, xxii, 93
  persistence of authoritarianism in, xx
  stability of authoritarian regime in, 125
  state capacity of, xxi
Rwandan Patriotic Front (RPF), 80, 91–93, 100*b*

**S**
Al Said, Jamshib bin Abdulla, 26*b*
Samba-Panza, Catherine, 24*b*
Saro-Wiwa, Ken, 53
satire, as means of expression, 117
Saudi Arabia
  engagement with African states, 127
  legislative representation of women in, 98*b*
school. *See* education
sectarianism, 26*b*
segregation. *See* apartheid
Senegal
  colonial rule in, 7, 10*b*
  economic independence from foreign aid, 120
  as one-party state, 30
  political rights in, xxiv*b*
Senghor, Léopold Sédar, xxvi, 7, 12–13*b*, 43, 76*b*
settler colonialism, 8*b*, 22
sexism, 13
sexual minorities, 102
Sharpeville massacre (1960), 22
single-party states. *See* one-party states
Sisulu, Walter, 36
Smith, Ian, 54, 68–69*b*
Soares de Oliveira, Ricardo, 46
socialism, 19–20, 26*b*, 37*b*, 61, 62, 69*b*
Sokoto Caliphate, 9
Somalia
  Cold War international relations, 63–65*b*
  communist regime in, 61–62
  foreign aid to, 62
  legitimizing narratives in, 32
  peacekeeping interventions in, 78

South Africa
  apartheid in, 16, 22, 35–36, 41, 42
  economic independence from
    foreign aid, 120
  freedom movement in, 35, 36, 37–40*b*
  independence of, 35
South Sudan, nationalism in, xxiii
Soviet Union. *See also* Cold War
  collapse of, 65, 70
  foreign aid from, 68
state-building activities, 16, 46, 80, 103
state capacity, xxi, 16, 90, 102
states
  border determination for, 14–15
  colonial, 5–6, 14, 16
  democratic framework for, 4
  gatekeeper, 48, 52*b*, 57
  masculine idea of, 28
  one-party (*see* one-party states)
  petro-states, 46, 57, 58*b*
  surveillance, xvii
Stepan, Alfred, xxvi
structural adjustment programs, 55
Sudan
  ethnic cleansing in, xxiv*b*
  foreign aid to, 80
  humor as means of expression in, 117
  legitimizing narratives in, xxiii
  oil industry in, 48
  state capacity of, xxi
sultanistic regimes, xxvi
surveillance states, xvii
Swaziland
  legislative representation of women in, 102
  public attitudes toward democracy in, 109

**T**
Tanganyika African National Union (TANU),
    30
Tanzania
  democratic backsliding in, 125
  economic growth in, 90, 91*f*
  foreign aid to, 69*b*
  legitimizing narratives in, 21, 32
  nationalism in, xxiii, 31
  natural gas reserves in, 125
  oil imports in, 53
  as one-party state, 30, 31
  political education in, 111, 112*b*
  political rights in, xxiv*b*, 24
  *ujamaa* philosophy in, 30, 31
terrorism, 62, 79
Tewodros II (Ethiopia), 20
Thiong'o, Ngũgĩ wa, 41
Togo

colonial rule in, 10*b*
  national conferences held in, 71
Tolbert, William, 76*b*
Tombalbaye, François, 76*b*
torture, 41, 83, 88
totalitarian regimes, xxvi, 16
Touré, Ahmed Sékou, 32, 33*b*, 67, 68
trade unions, 21–24, 31, 47, 55, 71, 74
traditional leaders. *See* chiefs
Trump, Donald
  "make America great again" strategy, 127
  career of, 46
Trump, Ivanka, 45–46
Tsvangirai, Morgan, 114
Ture, Samori, 32
Tutsi community, 91–93

**U**
Uganda
  anti-homosexuality legislation in, 102
  disabled persons in, 98
  foreign aid to, 66, 78–79
  invasion of Rwanda, 91
  Iraq War supported by, 79
  legislative representation of women in, 99*b*
  legitimizing narratives in, xxiii, xxiv, 93–94
  military regimes in, 28–31
  no-party democracy in, xxiv, 31
  oil finds in, 125
  policing of women's bodies in, 28
  public attitudes toward democracy in, 109
  state capacity of, xxi
  sultanism in, xxvi
Uganda People's Congress, 77*b*
unions. *See* trade unions
United Kingdom
  colonial rule by, 10–11*b*, 67
  coups supported by, 25–26*b*
  foreign aid from, xxi
  legislative representation of women in, 98*b*
  multiparty politics in, 24
  on political conditionality, 72*b*
  pressure for political change from, 84
  shifts in democracy promotion, 127
  trade with Africa, 53, 68–69*b*
United National Independence Party (UNIP),
    53, 55, 56, 74, 77*b*
United Nations
  on colonial rule, 7
  Committee Against Torture, 82–83
  General Assembly, 78
  trade sanctions from, 68*b*
United States. *See also* Cold War
  containment policy of, 68, 68–69*b*
  coups supported by, 25–26*b*

United States (*continued*)
  electoral college in, 116
  foreign aid from, xxi, 62, 68
  in Iraq War, 79
  legislative representation of women in, 98*b*
  multiparty politics in, 24
  peacekeeping interventions by, 78
  on political conditionality, 72*b*
  pressure for political change from, 84
  shifts in democracy promotion, 127
  trade with Africa, 53
unity. *See also* nationalism
  as justification for coups, 25, 26*b*
  language of, 31, 85
  in legitimizing narratives, 31, 32
  in one-party states, xxiii, 30–31, 34–35, 101
  as priority for African societies, 111
  promotion through education, 30
Uwilingiyimana, Agathe, 23–24*b*

**V**
Van de Walle, Nicolas, 103
violence
  civil wars, 14, 24*b*, 30, 46, 59, 69*b*
  genocide, xxiv*b*, 66, 78, 92, 93
  in military regimes, 28
  political, 8*b*, 14, 75, 114–115, 120
  *Qey Shibir* (Ethiopian Red Terror), 21, 69
  Sharpeville massacre (1960), 22
  suppression of dissent through, xxv, 21,
    82–83, 89
  torture, 41, 83, 88
  in wars of liberation, 11*b*

**W**
Wang, Vibeke, 99*b*
Weber, Max, xxvi
"Which Way Nigeria" (Okuson), 58*b*
white minority governments, 22, 35,
  53–54, 68*b*
white supremacy, 35
winner-takes-all politics, 14

women
  authoritarian leadership by, 23–24*b*
  in colonial period, 13, 31
  economic advancement for, 28
  femocracy and, 99*b*
  gender equality for, 98, 98–100*b*, 102
  legislative representation of, 98–100*b*, 102
  marginalization of, 13, 101–102
  policing of bodies of, 28
  political rights for, 4
  response to political violence, 114–115, *115*
  sexism and, 13
*Women Who Work* (Trump), 45–46
World Bank, xxi, 55, 56, 74, 78

**Z**
Zaïre. *See* Democratic Republic of Congo
Zambia
  colonial rule in, 7, 10–11*b*
  copper industry in, 54–55
  democratic backsliding in, 125
  education in, 7
  elections in, 73, 73*f*
  foreign aid to, 69*b*
  multiparty politics in, 53, 56
  nationalism in, xxiii
  as one-party state, 30, 53, 55–56, 73
  political rights in, xxiv*b*, 24, 73
  public attitudes toward democracy in, 109
  trade unions in, 55, 74
zero-sum politics, 14
Zimbabwe
  democratic backsliding in, 124
  foreign aid to, 80
  independence of, 68*b*
  informal settlements in, 114, 118
  legitimizing narratives in, xxiii
  persistence of authoritarianism in, xx
  political violence in, 114–115, 120
  settler colonialism in, 8*b*, 22
  trade sanctions against, 68–69*b*
Zulu Kingdom, 9